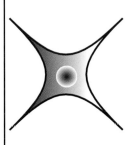

The Bible Explorer

Written by
Carine Mackenzie

Illustrated by
Jeff Anderson

Published by
Christian Focus Publications

Copyright information:

Additional contributors:

Cover Design
Owen Daily

Photographic Material:
Christian Focus Publications gratefully acknowledges the cooperation of these sources, whose illustrations appear in the present work -
Bible Scene Multimedia;
Threes Company;
Israeli Government Tourist Office;
Ewen Weatherspoon; Fin Macrae.
Cartographers: Ian Messider and Linda Swanson,
LAS Cartographic Services.
Computer picture of Temple: Neil Stewart.

Note from the author:

Many people have helped with the production of this book. I would like particularly to thank Catherine Mackenzie, the children's editor, Jeff Anderson the artist, Marianne Ross who worked on the manuscript, and the whole CFP team who have given suggestions and encouragement at every stage.

The Bible Explorer

Presented to:

....

From:

....

Date:

....

Oh, how I love your law! I meditate on it all day long.
Your commands make me wiser than my enemies, for they
are ever with me. I have more insight than all my teachers,
for I meditate on your word. I have more understanding than
the elders, for I obey your laws (Psalm 119:97-100).

The Bible Explorer

Introduction Pack

The Bible is a very special book. It is God's message to us. God tells us about himself and how we ought to live. The Bible was written by many people over a period of 1,500 years yet because God inspired each writer, the whole book has a unity. God is the author.

The Bible is divided into two sections:
The Old Testament and The New Testament.

The Old Testament has 39 books
originally written in the Hebrew language.
The New Testament has 27 books
originally written in Greek.

Each book is divided into chapters. Each chapter is divided into verses. This makes it easier for us to find a specific sentence in the book.

Psalm 19

David tells us in Psalm 19 that God's Word is

* Perfect   * Trustworthy
* Right   * Radiant
* Pure   * Sure
* Precious

Agur in the book of Proverbs chapter 30 tells us that God's Word is flawless. Jesus tells us that the Bible, or Scriptures, are reliable and have authority. "The Scripture cannot be broken," (John 10:35).

Paul tells us in the second letter to Timothy that the whole Bible is God-breathed or inspired by God (2 Timothy 3:16).

Jesus praying to God the Father affirms that God's Word is truth (John 17:17).

The Bible Explorer

Layout

Welcome to *The Bible Explorer*. We hope that you will enjoy this adventure, exploring God's word and finding out what God has to say to you personally. Before you begin the exploration please take time to read the introduction pack which is full of information to help you along your way. Note that at the top of each page there is a menu bar like this:

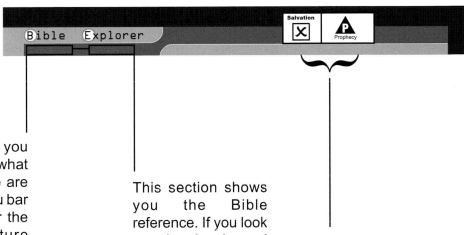

In the first section you will see at a glance what part of scripture we are exploring. The menu bar shows you whether the passage of scripture comes from The Old Testament or The New Testament. It also tells you whether it is Law, History, Poetry, Prophecy, Gospels, or Letters.

This section shows you the Bible reference. If you look up the book and chapters mentioned here you will be able to read the stories, law or poetry for yourself in God's word.

This section is the Link section and is a special feature of *The Bible Explorer*. When you look at this part of the page you will see at a glance what themes are being dealt with on the particular page that you are reading. For further information about the themes and links covered in *The Bible Explorer* go to the next page.

The Bible Explorer

What are the different themes you should look out for in *The Bible Explorer*? We have picked several different themes for you to research. Each theme has its own icon. The themes that are covered in this book are: *Prayer, Salvation, Prophecy, Animals and Emotions*. Under each icon you are told where that theme is mentioned next.

So for example page 15 has an animal icon on it. Underneath this icon you will read "Page 16". This means if you want to read another story that mentions animals you should turn to page 16.

As well as reading this book from cover to cover you can also dip in and read up on the different themes that interest you.

Try following all the different themes throughout the book at different times. The themes of Salvation and Prophecy are very good ones to explore further. To get you ready for this exploration adventure here are the different icons you will be looking out for:

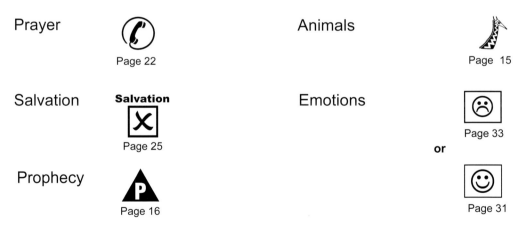

Prayer	Animals
Page 22	Page 15
Salvation	Emotions
Page 25	Page 33
	or
Prophecy	
Page 16	Page 31

Another icon that you should look out for is our special Explorer icon.

Explorer Icon
Page 46

One thing that you will notice as you read this book is how one Bible story has connections with another. For example in the story of Ruth we read that she was allowed to gather corn in Boaz's field. The reason she could do this was because many years before God had given the Israelites laws about how to treat the poor. So when you see the Explorer icon in Ruth's story it will show you where to go to find out a little more information about this law.

Fact File

Look out for features like these. This is a fact file and you will find one on almost every page where there are interesting facts to find out and investigate. Perhaps you want to know how big the ark was and why it was that the raven never came back but the dove did? That is why the fact files are here... to give you just that sort of information.

Think Spot

Every page has a Think Spot. This is to help you think further about important lessons from God's Word, the Bible. The Bible is more than a collection of stories. It is God's Word written for the people of the world, including you. It is relevant for your life. It is important that you obey it.

Memory Verse

On every page there is a Memory verse to read and learn. Memorising scripture is important. Learning scriptures by heart will help you in whatever situation you find yourself. Whether you are in difficulties or things are going very well for you, God's word always has something to say to you. Memorising God's word in your heart and mind will help you to remember God's instructions for your life.

You will come across several coloured boxes throughout *The Bible Explorer*. Keep a look out for them as these boxes highlight particular parts of a story or Bible verses - for example, The Ten Plagues in Egypt on page 38 or the Beatitudes on page 118.

Contents Page

Old Testament Overview

LAW

Genesis

The first book in the Bible and the first book of Moses. We are introduced to the story of creation and the fall or how God made the world and how sin destroyed it.

Exodus

The second book of Moses tells of the departure of the Israelites from Egypt.

Leviticus

This book is the third book of Moses. It deals with Tabernacles and Feasts.

Numbers

This book is the fourth book of Moses. It was written when the Israelites were in the wilderness.

Deuteronomy

This is the fifth book of Moses. Joshua succeeds Moses as leader.

HISTORY

Joshua

An historical book. It tells of the campaign to win the land of Canaan under the leadership of Joshua.

Judges

A book of stories of Israelite heroes called Judges. It is an historical book that teaches us to follow God.

Ruth

The events that take place in this book occur at the end of the age of the Judges. It is the story of Ruth, the Moabitess and her mother-in-law Naomi.

1 & 2 Samuel

Samuel was a Hebrew prophet and judge. The books in the Bible named after him tell of his life and of the two Israelite Kings he anointed – Saul and David.

1 & 2 Kings

History of the kings of Israel starting with Solomon, and then the kings of the divided kingdom of Israel and Judah. It also tells of the prophets of that time, Elijah, Micaiah and Elisha.

1 & 2 Chronicles

Covers the same period of time as 1st and 2nd Kings and some of 2nd Samuel. A religious history of the Jewish people.

Ezra

The fifteenth book of the Old Testament tells of the return of the Jews from Babylonian captivity.

Nehemiah

Written like a diary this book tells of the Jews' return from Babylonian captivity.

Esther

The story of Queen Esther and the Jewish people in Persia under King Xerxes.

POETRY

Job

The story of a man named Job, his trials and his trust in God.

Psalms

A book of praises written by David and others like Moses, Solomon and Asaph. Includes psalms of thanks, repentance and sorrow as well as psalms that foretell the coming of Christ.

Proverbs

Tells us what to think about God and how to live wisely as well as giving instruction to young people.

Ecclesiastes

A book of wisdom written by someone referred to as 'The Teacher'. This book takes a look at life and concludes that human wisdom, achievement, power, wealth and pleasure are all meaningless.

Song of Solomon

A love song expressing the love of a bridegroom and his bride.

PROPHECY

Major Prophets
Isaiah, Jeremiah, Lamentations, Ezekiel, Daniel.

Direct messages from God to the people of Israel and Judah through men called prophets. The major prophets wrote long books. We learn about the lives of the prophets too.

Minor Prophets
Hosea, Joel, Amos, Obadiah, Jonah, Micah, Nahum, Habbakuk, Zephaniah, Haggai, Zechariah, Malachi.

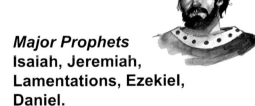

Messages from God through the prophets. They are called minor prophets because the messages are shorter but not less important.

In the Beginning

The first words of the Bible are 'In the beginning God...' God has existed always. He did not have a beginning and he will have no end. He is not limited by time. He is eternal. He is not limited by space. He is present everywhere. He is unchanging. He is the same every day. He knows everything and has all things in his power. He is wise, holy, just and good.

It is hard for us to grasp all the wonderful truths about God but he has told us such a lot about himself and we can learn it from his book the Bible.

God created the world and everything that is in it from nothing. God is all-powerful.

He spoke a few words and the different parts of creation came into being.

On the first day, God created light. He said, 'Let there be light,' and the light appeared immediately. God thought the light was good. He separated it from the darkness. He called the light "Day" and the darkness "Night".

On the second day God made the atmosphere - the sky with all the different kinds of clouds. God made all the water in the earth too - the oceans, rivers, ponds and underground springs. Every drop of water was made by God.

On the third day God spoke and dry land appeared. Hills and valleys, plains and mountains were created by his power. He made trees, bushes, plants and flowers – all producing seed so that the vegetation would reproduce and spread. God saw that what he had made was good.

On the fourth day God made the sun and moon and the stars. 'Let there be lights in the sky. May they be forces to give order to the seasons and the days and years,' he said. God was pleased with his creation. On the fifth day God made sea creatures and birds.

Fact File

Genesis: The first book in the Bible. Introduces the story of creation and the fall or how God made the world and how sin entered the world.

Eternal: This word means to last for ever. To have eternal life means to live for ever. Although the body dies, if a person believes in Jesus they will live forever with God in heaven.

Salvation
Page 15

1

2

3

4

'Let the waters be filled with living creatures and let the birds fly across the sky,' said God.

So the fish and the shrimp and the shark were made by God. The little robin and the magnificent eagle were created by God's power.

On the sixth day God made the animals.

Page 15

'Let the land produce living creatures,' he said.

So God made the horse and the monkey, the sheep and the elephant - every kind of animal.

Then God came to the best part of his creation - the first person.

5

6

God Made Adam and Eve

"Let us make man in our own image," God said. "Man will rule over the fish in the sea and the birds in the air and over all the animals and creeping things."

The Lord God made a man from the dust on the ground. He breathed the breath of life into his nostrils and man became a living soul. The man was called Adam. God did not want Adam to be alone so he made a woman to be a help and companion for him. He caused Adam to fall into a very deep sleep. While he was sleeping, God took one of Adam's ribs then closed the flesh again. From this rib God made a woman called Eve. Adam was very glad. "She is part of me," he said, "bone of my bone and flesh of my flesh."

God blessed Adam and Eve. He told them to have children and rule over all the other living creatures. God gave them a beautiful garden to live in with plants and fruits to eat. Adam had the task of giving names to all the animals - to show he was in charge of them all.

Fact File

Sin: This is doing, saying or thinking what displeases God or not doing, saying or thinking what God requires. He tells us in his Word what we ought to do. Every time we disobey God it is sin.

The seventh day: God rested on the seventh day called the Sabbath. The Lord's Day or Sunday is the special day for us to keep holy.

Page 42

Fact File God saw that everything he had made was very good. He rested from all his work on the seventh day and made this day of the week very special.

Sin Spoils the World

God gave Adam and Eve the beautiful Garden of Eden to live in. There were lovely trees with delicious fruit to eat. Adam's work was to look after the garden. "You are free to eat from any tree," God said, "except the tree of the knowledge of good and evil which is in the middle of the garden. If you eat fruit from that tree, you will die."

Page 48 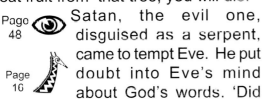 Satan, the evil one, disguised as a serpent, came to tempt Eve. He put Page 16 doubt into Eve's mind about God's words. 'Did God really say that you must not eat from one tree in the garden?" he asked.

"Yes," Eve replied. "We can eat from any tree except the one in the middle which we must not touch or we will die."

Satan then lied to Eve. "You will not die," he said. "God knows that if you eat that fruit your eyes will be opened and you will know good and evil, like God."

Eve listened to Satan's lies. She looked at the forbidden fruit, took some and ate it. She gave some to Adam and he ate it too. Sin entered the world. Adam and Eve were no longer innocent. They realised that they were naked and felt ashamed. They sewed fig leaves together to try to make clothes to cover themselves.

God's Wonderful Creation: When we look at God's creation today it reminds us of what a wonderful God we have. When you think about God's creation remember how God rested on the seventh day. We should do this too.

Sin: The effects of sin can be seen everywhere and not just in barren landscapes and dry deserts. Sin is seen in the lives and hearts of human beings. Murders, wars, fighting, famines, droughts and disease, illness and death are all a result of mankind's sinful nature. But Jesus Christ has come to set us free. Take a look at the think spot.

 **Think Spot** Were Adam and Eve stupid to sin? Think about when you give into temptation. You are no better than Adam and Eve.

But remember God is there to help you fight temptation and you can ask for forgiveness through Jesus Christ.

Salvation [X] Page 16

 Memory Verse

All have sinned and fall short of the glory of God (Romans 3:23).

Sin must be punished

Adam and Eve knew that they had been disobedient. When they heard God walking in the garden in the cool of the day, they hid among the trees because they were afraid. "Where are you, Adam?" God called.

Adam could not hide from God. The sin was found out. Adam blamed Eve. Eve blamed the serpent but God has to punish sin. He spoke first to the serpent, "You are more cursed than any other creature. You will crawl on the ground all your life. You will

Page 18

Salvation

Fact File

eat dust. There will be enmity between you and the woman, between your children and hers. The woman's son will crush your head and you will hurt his heel."

Eve too was punished. "You will have pain when you give birth to a child. You will be dependant on your husband. He will rule over you." Adam's punishment was then handed out. "You will work hard all your life. The ground will not be easy to work any more. Thorns and

Fact File

thistles will make it difficult. You will produce food to eat but the hard work will make you sweat. You were made from the dust and you will return to the dust one day."

God in that way told Adam that he would die. God made clothes from animal skins for Adam and Eve - then sent them away from the beautiful garden for ever.

Cain and Abel

Adam and Eve had a baby son and they called him Cain. Then his brother Abel was born. When they grew up, Abel became a shepherd, while Cain cultivated the land. One day both young men brought offerings to the Lord. Cain brought the produce of his field and Abel brought one of his best animals. God was pleased with Abel's offering but Cain's offering was not as God required.

Fact File

Promise of a Saviour: When God punished the serpent, he gave Adam and Eve hope for the future in spite of their sin. He promised them salvation and that the devil would be defeated. The New Testament teaches us that Jesus fulfills these promises. This victory was not without pain and suffering for him.

Salvation

See Think Spot

P Fulfilment on Pages 138 & 139

Adam and Eve's Children: Adam and Eve were distressed when they saw what sin had done to the lives of Cain and Abel, their sons, and to realise that one of their children had murdered the other. Adam and Eve lost both their sons because of sin. Abel was murdered and Cain was driven out. However, later on, Eve gave birth to another son, and his name was Seth.

Thorns and Weeds: These make gardening and farming difficult for us today. This is one of the direct results of sin.

See Paragraph on Adam's Punishment

Cain was angry with God and with his brother. When the brothers were out in the field, Cain killed his brother Abel. God confronted Cain. "Where is Abel your brother?" he asked. "I do not know," lied Cain. "Am I my brother's keeper?"

Page 42

God knew what Cain had done. Cain was cursed by God. He was driven out from the land and forced to wander about all his life. Cain became afraid that he would be killed himself. God put a special mark on Cain so that no one who found him would kill him.

 **Think Spot**

God accepted Abel's offering but it wasn't perfect. This type of offering was meant as a picture of a better offering or sacrifice to come. Jesus Christ offered up his life as a perfect sacrifice. When Jesus died on the cross his sacrifice was so perfect no other sacrifices are needed. Salvation is now free to all who believe in the name of Jesus Christ.

Salvation ☒ See Memory Verse

 Memory Verse

Salvation ☒

Page 18

The sting of death is sin... But thanks be to God! He gives us the victory through our Lord Jesus Christ (1 Corinthians 15:56-57).

The Flood

Abel's murder was the very first murder but it wasn't the last. The people of the earth became more and more evil. God was so grieved with them that he decided to send a flood to destroy all that was bad. Only Noah and his family would be saved because Noah was a just man and pleased God.

Next paragraph

God gave Noah detailed instructions to build a large boat called an ark. Two of every animal, male and female, and seven of some, were taken into the ark with enough food for a long stay. Noah, his wife, and three sons, Shem, Ham and Japheth and their wives went into the ark with the animals as God had commanded. Then God shut the door. The rain began to fall and it rained continuously for forty days and nights, flooding the earth and destroying all the wicked people.

Water covered the whole earth for 150 days. When the water began to recede, the ark came to rest on Mount Ararat. Once Noah could see the mountain tops again, he sent out a raven and a dove from the ark. The raven did not return but the dove came back for she could not find a resting place. Seven days later Noah sent out the dove again. This time the dove returned with an olive leaf in her mouth. Noah knew that the tree tops had appeared again.

Page 20

Think Spot

What do you think about sin? Is it serious or not? Sin is very serious in God's eyes. All sin deserves God's anger. Jesus Christ was sinless yet he suffered the full anger of God because of sin. This means that those who follow him can live in eternal peace with God.

Salvation

See Page 21

Memory Verse

Noah did everything just as God commanded him (Genesis 6:22).

After another seven days Noah sent out the dove once more and this time she did not return. When the earth was completely dry, God told Noah to take his wife and family and the animals out of the ark.

Noah built an altar and offered a burnt offering to God as an act of worship and thankfulness for sparing him and his family. God promised that he would never again destroy the earth with a flood. God made the rainbow as a sign of the covenant or promise he made with Noah.

Fact File

Ravens and Doves: The Raven is a carnivore. It eats flesh. It could have survived on dead animals floating on the water. The dove is a herbivore. They eat plants and leaves. It could not survive until the trees were showing above the water.

Rainbow: A sign of God's covenant that he would never flood the whole earth again.

Ark's Dimensions: The ark was designed for stability – 140 metres long, over 23 metres wide, 13.5 metres high.

Covenant: This is a gracious promise made by God to Noah and every living creature.

See Page 20

Abraham and Sarah

Page 21

Abraham and his family lived in the land of Mesopotamia. Abraham owned many sheep and cows, donkeys and camels. He was wealthy. His wife Sarah was very beautiful, but she had no children.

One day God spoke to Abraham, "Leave your home and go to another land. I will show you where to go."

Abraham and Sarah made a long journey, living in a tent, always obeying God's leading.

God made a covenant with Abraham, "I will make your family into a great nation. I will bless you. All the people in the world will be blessed through you."

Abraham and Sarah were nomads. This means that they travelled from place to place with their animals in order to find pasture. The picture here shows a typical example of a tent that a nomadic family might live in today.

When they reached the land of Canaan, God said, "I will give this land to your children."

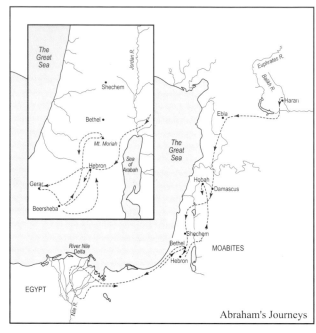

Abraham's Journeys

This was an amazing promise as Abraham and Sarah still had no sons and they were both growing old. Abraham built an altar and worshipped God there.

One of Abraham's travelling companions was his nephew Lot. They both owned many animals.

Fact File

Covenant: A gracious promise made by God to Abraham - and Noah.

Page 19

Altars: Usually made of earth or stone. Animals were offered on them as an act of worship to God.

Tents: Abraham and his family lived in tents made of animal skins or cloth supported by poles.

Names: Abraham was originally called Abram and Sarah, Sarai. God gave them new names to show how he would bless them. Abraham means, father of many nations and Sarah means mother of nations.

Fact File Pages 22 & 30

Page 24
 Soon the herdsmen began to quarrel. It was difficult to find enough grass for all the animals. Abraham said to Lot, "We should not be fighting. We are brothers. Let's go to different parts of the country. You choose which way you want to go and I will go the other way."
Page 22

Lot chose the fruitful plains of Jordan to the east near the wicked city of Sodom. This led to many problems for Lot. Abraham and Sarah went in the other direction. God reminded Abraham of his promise, "You and your children will possess this land. You will have so many descendants that it will be hard to count them."

Salvation

Page 23

Abraham worshipped God again. God's promise to Abraham points to the Lord Jesus Christ. Jesus was descended from the family of Abraham. The world is blessed through him.

 **Think Spot**

Abraham showed great faith in following God's command to leave his home and family.

Even today some people who love God, obey him by travelling to other countries to spread the good news of Jesus Christ.

Remember to pray for some of these people today.

Memory Verse

The Lord is faithful to all his promises (Psalm 145:13).

Isaac and Ishmael

God promised Abraham a son, and many descendants in the future. But as he and Sarah, his wife, grew older, still no child arrived. Sarah was impatient and told Abraham to take her maid servant Hagar as his wife. This was not God's command and led to trouble and jealousy in the family when Hagar did have a son, Ishmael. Ishmael was not God's promised child. Again God spoke to Abraham, "Sarah will have a son." Abraham laughed. How could Sarah have a baby at 90 years of age?

One day as Abraham sat at the door of his tent, he noticed three men approaching. Welcoming them to his tent, he allowed them to rest and wash. Then he gave them a fine meal.

They were no ordinary visitors. They were God's messengers. "This time next year," they said, "Sarah will have a son." When Sarah overheard that, she laughed. God rebuked her, "Is anything too hard for the Lord?"

God kept his promise. Isaac was born when Abraham was 100 and Sarah was 90. Nothing is too hard for God. Abraham had believed God's promise and his faith was rewarded. But there was trouble between Sarah and Hagar and their sons Isaac and Ishmael.

Page 27

Ishmael made fun of the younger Isaac. Sarah was angry and jealous. "Get rid of that slave woman," she demanded. Abraham was reluctant to do so but God encouraged him. Isaac was the child of the promise not Ishmael. Ishmael and Hagar were sent away to the desert. They got into trouble when their water ran out but God looked after them. God heard Ishmael crying and just in time he showed Hagar a well of water. Ishmael survived. He became an archer and was the father of a mighty nation called the Ishmaelites.

Page 24

Fact File

Meaning of names: Abraham - father of many nations; *Sarah* - Fact File Page 20 mother of nations; *Isaac* - laughter

Bottle: Water container made out of animals skins. Page 24

God Tested Abraham's Faith

"Take your son Isaac, whom you love," said God, "to Mount Moriah. Sacrifice him there as an offering to me."

Abraham believed God. He obeyed him faithfully. Early in the morning Abraham and Isaac set off with two servants and plenty of wood.

Isaac was puzzled that there was fire and wood but no lamb for the offering. "God will provide the lamb," said his father. So father and son continued up the mountain. Abraham built an altar and placed wood on it. He tied Isaac's hands and feet and laid him on top of the wood. He believed God was in charge. He raised the knife, ready to kill Isaac. Then the angel of the Lord called out, "Abraham, Abraham."

"Here I am," he replied.

"Do not harm the boy," the angel said. "I know that you fear God, because you were willing to sacrifice your son." Abraham then noticed a ram caught in a bush by its horns. This was used as a sacrifice. God had provided a lamb for a sacrifice. Again Abraham was reminded of the blessing.

Salvation
Think Spot

Think Spot

Salvation
Memory Verse

Abraham was willing to sacrifice his son but did not have to. God, the Father, sacrificed his only son Jesus on the cross at Calvary.

 Memory Verse

Christ was sacrificed once to take away the sins of many people (Hebrews 9:28).

Salvation
Page 25

A Bride for Isaac

Abraham wanted his son to marry a woman from his native land of Mesopotamia. He sent his most trusted servant to find her. The servant prayed that God would guide him to the right person.

Page 26

Rebekah was a beautiful girl. She was a good and dutiful daughter who helped her father Bethuel and her mother with the household tasks. One of her daily duties was to fetch water for the house from the well. One evening she met a stranger at the well.

Fact File

Rebekah kindly gave him a refreshing drink of water and also drew enough water for his camels to drink. This was a huge job.

The stranger, who was in fact Abraham's servant, believed his prayer had been answered.

When he discovered that this kind girl, Rebekah, was of the same family as his master Abraham, he was sure that she was the wife for Isaac. Arrangements were made with Rebekah's family and she agreed to make the long journey with the servant to a strange land to meet Isaac. They were married when Isaac was forty years old.

How much water can a camel drink? See the fact file.

Water bottle

Water was very important to travellers in Bible times. They needed water for their animals and themselves. If you run out of water in a hot, dry, climate you will fall ill, very quickly, and can even die from thirst. The picture here shows a water bottle. This would have been used in Bible times to carry water.

Page 22

Fact File

Marriage: It was not unusual for people to marry someone chosen for them by someone else. In Isaac's time marriage was often organised by a young person's parents.

Camel: A single camel can drink up to 25 gallons, about 100 litres. Abraham's servant had 10 camels, so they would have needed about 1,000 litres of water.

Page 28

Twins

Isaac and Rebekah were married for nearly twenty years but they still had no child. Isaac prayed to God and asked him to give them a baby. God answered his prayer and Rebekah was soon expecting not one baby but twins. God told Rebekah that her boys would be two different nations and that the younger one would be more important than the older one. When the twins were born they looked very different. Esau was born first. He was red and hairy. Jacob, his brother, was smooth skinned.

As they grew up they were different in nature too. Esau was a rugged outdoor man. He loved hunting which greatly pleased his father. Jacob preferred the quieter pursuits around the home. He was his mother's favourite.

 The servant's prayer was for guidance. We too can ask God to guide us in decisions and choices. What is the most important choice you have to make? Is it what job you will do? Is it where you are going to live or what you are going to spend your money on?

These are all important choices but the most important one is to choose to love and obey Jesus Christ.

Salvation

Memory Verse

 Memory Verse

God will be our guide, even to the end (Psalm 48:14).

Salvation

Page 27

Esau's Birthright

As the older son Esau had the right to certain privileges called the birthright. This included a double share of the inheritance and the right to be the head of the family.

One day Esau came in from hunting. He was absolutely ravenous. Jacob had been cooking and Esau could smell the lovely lentil stew. "Give me some of that stew," he asked, "I am about to faint with hunger."

"I'll give you some food," replied Jacob, "if you give me your birthright."

"What use is a birthright to me, if I die of hunger?" said Esau.

So the agreement was made. Jacob had the birthright and Esau received some bread and lentil stew. The birthright did not seem to be of importance to Esau.

Jacob's Blessing

Page 29

Isaac wanted to pray especially for his elder son and heir, asking for God's blessing or favour. To be blessed is to be truly happy. This happiness is given by God.

Rebekah overheard a conversation one day between old blind Isaac and his son Esau. Isaac was planning to give Esau his blessing and told him to go out hunting and bring back some venison for his favourite meal.

Fact File

Asking for a Blessing: When someone asks God for favour on themselves or another person

Birthright: The right of the first born to inherit the father's blessing and a double share of the inheritance. They also assumed headship of the family when the father died.

Rebekah and Jacob worked out a trick. Rebekah quickly made a dish of goat stew, tasting like venison. Jacob dressed in Esau's clothes and put the young goat skins on his smooth hands and neck. He felt and smelt like Esau now. Jacob then lied to his father and tricked him into thinking he was Esau. Isaac blessed Jacob, asking God to provide for him and make him prosper.

Think Spot

Esau was so angry when he returned too late. He had lost the blessing as well as the birthright. He vowed to kill Jacob.

Think Spot

Jealousy and feuding lead to stress and heartache. Deal with this by following God's advice. Look at the memory verse. Remember also that Jesus tells us to forgive people and love our enemies. When he was on the cross to save his people from their sins he even forgave the people who were hurting him. Jesus is the best example for us to follow.

Memory Verse

Salvation

Page 29

Memory Verse

Do not let the sun go down while you are still angry (Ephesians 4:26).

Page 29

Bible Explorer

Jacob's Adventures at Bethel

When Rebekah heard that Esau planned to kill Jacob she urged him to escape to his Uncle Laban's place. Jacob never saw his mother again.

One night Jacob lay down in the open air with a big stone as his pillow. As he slept he dreamt that he saw a ladder going from earth to heaven and angels were going up and down it. God spoke to him in the dream as he had spoken to Abraham.

"I am the God of Abraham and Isaac: I will give you this land: you and your children will be blessed." Jacob woke up, afraid and full of awe. "This is surely the house of God and the gate of heaven." He named the place where he had seen the vision "Bethel" meaning "House of God".

Early next morning, Jacob took the stone that had been his pillow, set it up as a pillar and poured oil on it. He made a vow to follow the Lord and give him one tenth of all his income.

Jacob's Adventures at Haran

As Jacob drew near his Uncle Laban's home, he stopped at a well where he met Rachel, Laban's daughter. Jacob helped her to water her flock and introduced himself as Rebekah's son. Rachel ran to tell her father who was delighted to meet his nephew and welcomed him to his home. Jacob agreed to work for Laban for seven years as long as he could marry Rachel. Jacob loved the beautiful Rachel so much, that the seven years seemed a very short time.

Page 30

However, Jacob the trickster was tricked himself. The bride arrived, covered with a veil. When the veil was removed Jacob discovered that he had married Leah, Rachel's older sister. "Why did you deceive me?" he demanded.

"In our country the younger sister cannot get married before the older," insisted Laban. "You can marry Rachel too, if you work for another seven years."

Fact File

A vow: A solemn, binding promise.

Jacob did this and then wanted to return to Canaan with his family. Laban wasn't happy as Jacob did good work for him.

God told Jacob to return to the land of Canaan after his twenty years absence. "I will be with you," he promised. With God's help Jacob and his family, servants and animals journeyed towards Canaan.

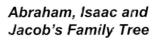 **Abraham, Isaac and Jacob's Family Tree**

Abraham and Sarah

Isaac and Rebekah

Jacob

Esau

 Page 32

 See Think Spot

Jacob was scared to go back to Canaan. He would meet Esau again. He prayed to God to keep him and his family safe.

 Rachel

 **Leah**

Bilhah and Zilpah: Rachel and Leah's maid servants

The twelve sons of Jacob

 **Think Spot**

We can pray for the safety of our family just as Jacob did. Our safety comes from God. It is a comfort to know that God is in control of everything that happens in our lives. Trusting in Jesus gives us safety for eternity.

 Page 30

Salvation Page 31

Memory Verse

For you alone, O Lord, make me dwell in safety (Psalm 4:8).

Presents for Esau

Jacob sent servants ahead with presents to give to Esau – 200 female goats, 20 male goats, 200 ewes, 20 rams, 30 camels with their colts, 40 cows, 10 bulls, 20 donkeys and 10 foals. What a gift!

Page 33

Page 31

"Tell him your servant Jacob is coming behind," he ordered. Jacob prayed for the safety of himself and his family.

A Struggle at Peniel

Jacob stayed that night alone in the camp at the brook Jabbok. A man appeared and wrestled with him until dawn. As they wrestled Jacob's hip was put out of joint.

"Let me go," the man said.

"I will not let you go unless you bless me," replied Jacob.

"Your name will no longer be Jacob, but Israel," said the man, "for you struggled with God and man and won."

Jacob realised that the stranger was God. He called the place Peniel because he had seen God face to face. After Jacob's encounter with God at Peniel he was left with a limp. This would always remind him of his meeting with God.

Fact File

Names: There are other examples of name changes in the Bible... Saul changed to Paul, Sarai to Sarah, Abram to Abraham...

Fact File
Page 20
& Page 145

Esau Comes Closer

Jacob divided his family into three groups – the maid servants and their children in front, Leah and her children, then Rachel and her son Joseph.

Page 35

See Think Spot

Jacob bowed down before Esau but Esau ran to him with open arms and welcomed him. All was forgiven. The brothers were reconciled and Jacob's family were introduced. They made their way safely to the land of Canaan. Jacob's prayer was answered.

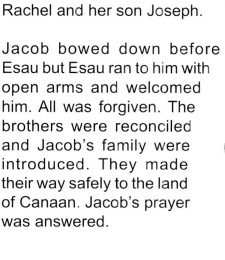

Think Spot

God answers prayer. What do you pray for? Can you give examples of answers to prayer? God sometimes answers, 'No' or 'Not yet'. These are still answers to prayer even though they may not be the answers that we want. The most important prayer is to ask for the forgiveness of our sins, because of the sacrifice of Jesus, God's beloved Son, who willingly gave his life on the cross for his people. This is God's salvation and it is a great and precious gift.

Page 36

Salvation

Page 33

 Memory Verse

O you who hear prayer, to you all men will come (Psalm 65:2).

Joseph at Home

Think Spot

Joseph lived in Canaan with his eleven brothers and one sister. Jacob gave Joseph, his favourite son, a coloured coat to show how much he loved him. The older brothers were jealous when they saw it. They hated Joseph, and spoke angrily to him. Joseph told them about his dream, "We were tying up corn in the field. My bundle stood straight, but yours all bowed down to mine." The brothers were angry. "Do you think that we will bow down to you one day?" they asked. Then Joseph had another dream. "The sun, the moon and eleven stars all bowed down to me." His brothers envied him more.

Page 35

Think Spot

Favouritism caused problems in Jacob's family. It led to jealousy which led to many other sins. When you feel jealous, ask God to help you to get rid of it.

Page 33

Memory Verse

He lifted me out of the slimy pit, out of the mud and mire; he set my feet on a rock and gave me a firm place to stand (Psalm 40:2).

Page
38

Even Jacob rebuked him. Then one day Jacob sent Joseph out to the countryside. "Go and visit your brothers who are looking after the sheep. Find out if they are all well and come back and tell me," instructed Jacob.

The brothers saw Joseph coming. "Let's kill him and throw his body in a pit. We can say a wild animal has eaten him." Reuben spoke up, "Don't kill him. Throw him into the pit, but don't harm him." So Joseph's beautiful coat was torn off and he was flung into a deep, dark, hole. Reuben secretly planned to rescue Joseph later and take him back to his father.

While Reuben was busy elsewhere a group of merchants came along, their camels loaded with

spices and perfumes to sell in Egypt. "Let's sell Joseph as a slave to these merchants," suggested Judah. "He is our brother after all. We had better not kill him." Joseph was pulled out of the pit and sold for 20 pieces of silver to the merchants. Reuben was upset when he came back to the pit to find

Next
Paragraph

Joseph gone. "What shall we do now?" he asked. A plan was hatched to deceive Jacob. The brothers killed a goat and dipped Joseph's coat in the blood. When Jacob saw the blood-stained coat he believed that a wild animal had torn Joseph to pieces. He was heart broken and could not be comforted.

Page 34

Fact File

Jacob's sons: Reuben, Simeon, Levi, Judah, Issachar, Zebulun, Joseph, Benjamin, Dan, Naphtali, Gad and Asher.

Coat of many colours: This was normally given to the oldest son or future head of the family. No wonder the brothers were jealous.

Pit: Joseph's brothers may have thrown him in a disused well. Look at the memory verse. It talks of being lifted out of a slimy pit. The Psalmist here is using the pit as a picture to describe what it is like to be trapped by sin. It is only the Lord Jesus Christ who can free us from the power of sin.

Salvation

Page 34

Joseph in Egypt

Joseph was still alive. He was sold by the merchants to an important official, Potiphar, a captain in the army of Pharaoh, the ruler of Egypt. God was with Joseph in this difficult situation. He worked well for his master and Potiphar rewarded him. Potiphar's wife made up a false story against Joseph, accusing him of a wicked deed that he had not done. But Potiphar believed his wife and Joseph was thrown into prison.

God was with Joseph in prison too. He was given a position of trust by the prison guards. Pharaoh's butler and baker were also in the prison. They both had a vivid dream one night. Only Joseph was able to tell them the meaning of the dreams. The butler would get his old job back, but the baker would be executed. Both dreams did come true.

"Tell Pharaoh about me," Joseph said to the butler as he went back to work in the palace, "I should not be in this prison."

However the butler forgot all about Joseph. Two years later Joseph was still in prison, but God was with him. One night Pharaoh had two dreams. He did not know what they meant, nor did his wise men. Pharaoh was worried. All of a sudden the butler remembered Joseph, and told Pharoah about him. Joseph was summoned to the palace. With God's help Joseph told Pharaoh the meaning of the dreams. There would be seven years of plenty in the land, followed by seven years of famine. Joseph gave Pharaoh good advice, "Find a wise man to

☹ Page 35

Fact File

Salvation: Many details of Joseph's life remind us of the life of the Lord Jesus. For example, Joseph was sent to Egypt in order to save his people from destruction by famine. The Lord Jesus was sent to this world to save his people from their sins.

Salvation

Think Spot

Pharoah: The title given to the ruler of Egypt, like King or Your Majesty.

oversee the storage of crops during the years of plenty so that there will be food for the people during the famine." Pharaoh gave this important job to Joseph. He became a ruler in the land of Egypt. Joseph did his job well. Huge storehouses kept the extra grain. During the famine when people looked for food, they were told, "Go to Joseph." They came from all over the land and even from the land of Canaan.

Page 32

One day Joseph's older brothers came to buy bread. They fell down before Joseph to ask for food, not realising who he was. The dream had come true.

Joseph did not tell them who he was at first. He insisted that young Benjamin be brought next time. He tested the brothers severely by hiding his silver cup in Benjamin's sack. When this was discovered, Judah begged Joseph to punish him instead of Benjamin. "It would kill his father if anything happened to him."

Joseph then had to tell them who he was. "I am Joseph your brother, whom you sold to Egypt. Do not be unhappy. God sent me here to save many lives and your lives."

Page 36

The brothers were sent back to fetch their father. What great news for Jacob – Joseph was still alive, the ruler of the land of Egypt. What a joyful reunion for Joseph and Jacob.

You can still see the monuments and architecture built by the ancient Egyptians. This picture shows a Pyramid in the background. Some of these Pyramids were built hundreds of years before Joseph's arrival in Egypt. However in the future the people of God would be used as slave labour to build other buildings and monuments for the Egyptians.

The brothers were afraid Joseph would turn against them after their father died, but Joseph could say, "You meant it to harm me, but God meant it for good and to save many lives."

Page 36

 Think Spot Isn't it wonderful how God used one person to save so many people? It's even more amazing how one man, Jesus Christ, died to save whoever believes in him.

Salvation
Page 36

 Memory Verse

In all things God works for the good of those who love him (Romans 8:28).

Moses

Next Column

Many years after Joseph's death another Pharaoh ruled in Egypt. He hated the Israelites who lived in his land. He was afraid that they would become powerful and fight him so he made them his slaves.

In Egypt at that time slaves did all the building work. They made bricks with water and earth mixed with chopped straw. This was then pressed into moulds. Pharoah forced the Israelites to make the bricks without giving them straw. They had to gather their own straw to make the bricks. It was back-breaking work. Pharaoh also gave the cruel order that all Israelite baby boys must be thrown into the River Nile.

An Israelite man called Amram and his wife Jochabed gave birth to a little boy. They already had a daughter, Miriam, and a son, Aaron. They hid the new baby in the house for three months. However, as he grew bigger he grew noisier and harder to hide.

So Jochabed thought of a plan. She made a basket of bulrushes and waterproofed it by coating it with tar. She put the baby in the basket and floated it at the water's edge among the reeds on the River Nile. Miriam stood guard. However, Pharoah's daughter came to bathe in the river and noticed the basket. But when she saw the baby crying she took pity on him. Miriam then suggested that she would fetch a nurse to look after the baby. The princess agreed. Miriam ran for her mother. Jochabed could now look after her son openly. The princess named him Moses, which means "drawn out of the water". When he was older, Moses went to live in the palace, but he never forgot that he was an Israelite. He worshipped the true God.

Page 61

When Moses was grown up, he saw an Egyptian beating an Israelite. He quickly looked round to see no one was watching, and then killed the Egyptian and buried the body in the sand. Another day he saw two Israelite men fighting and tried to stop them. One turned to Moses, "Do you mean to kill me just as you killed the Egyptian?"

Moses had been found out and he was scared. He fled to the land of Midian where he met Zipporah, who became his wife. While he was there the conditions in Egypt got even worse and the Israelites called out to God to help them. God had a plan to save them which involved Moses.

Page 38

Page 41

Fact File

Slaves: A slave is someone who is owned by a master and is purchased to do hard work or menial tasks. He has no freedom. The Bible tells us that by nature we are slaves to sin. Sin controls our lives. Christ Jesus freed his people from this slavery when he died on the cross.

Salvation

Page 39

Exodus: The second book of Moses, telling mainly of the departure from Egypt of the people of Israel.

The Burning Bush

Moses was looking after his father-in-law's sheep in the desert. He noticed a bush burning fiercely but the bush was not burnt up. "How strange," he thought. He went to see this great sight. God spoke from out of the bush and told Moses to go to Pharoah to ask him to let the people of Israel leave Egypt. God promised to be with him. Moses wasn't sure. God encouraged him by doing miraculous things.

"I cannot speak well," Moses objected.

"I will teach you what to say," said God.

Moses was still unwilling. "Aaron will help you to speak to Pharoah," God told him.

So Moses returned to Egypt.

 **Think Spot**

Moses was anxious about the task ahead. He did not feel able to do it. God encouraged him and gave him help. Remember this when you have a big problem. Ask God to help you.

 Memory Verse

Let us be thankful and so worship God acceptably with reverence and awe (Hebrews 12:28).

Bible Explorer

The Ten Plagues

Pharoah refused to let the people go. So God sent ten plagues to teach Pharoah a lesson. Firstly the River Nile was turned to blood. The river stank as all the fish died and no one could drink from the river. Pharaoh still refused to listen to God.

Then came a plague of frogs. Frogs were everywhere, even in Pharoah's palace. There wasn't a corner of any house that was free of frogs. A plague of lice came next and following that a plague of flies. Still Pharaoh refused to obey God's command and free the Israelites.

The fifth plague killed all the cattle and the sixth plague was a plague of festering boils that broke out on the skin of all the Egyptian people.

Horrific storms of hail stones were the seventh plague to afflict the nation of Egypt followed soon after by swarms of locusts. Pharaoh was very stubborn.

The ninth plague was when an unusually thick darkness covered the whole land for three whole days. The plagues seemed to get worse and worse. After the tenth plague Pharaoh finally begged the Israelites to leave. It was the worst one by far. The first born son in every Egyptian family died. There was great mourning in the country.

Page 40

The Ten Plagues
1. River Nile turned to blood
2. Frogs
3. Lice
4. Flies
5. Cattle diseased
6. Boils
7. Hail
8. Locusts
9. Darkness
10. Death of firstborn son

Page 42

The Passover

On the night before they left Egypt, the Israelites ate a feast of roast lamb with bitter herbs and bread without yeast. They ate it quickly standing up ready to leave. When they killed the lamb they took some blood and put it on the door posts and lintel of their homes. When the angel of death passed through the land killing all the firstborn sons, the homes with lamb's blood on the doorposts and lintel were passed over. That is why the feast was named the Passover feast.

Crossing the Red Sea

When Pharoah realised that his workforce had left - he sent chariots and soldiers to bring them back.

Fact File

Passover Feast: Jesus ate the Passover Feast with his disciples in the upper room, the night before he died on the cross. (Mark 14:12–26.)

Pages 134 & 135

However, at the Red Sea the waters parted and the Israelites walked across on dry land. They saw God's power and trusted in him. Pharoah's army raced towards the gap in the sea but when they were on the sea bed God caused their chariot wheels to come off. Moses stretched out his hand and the waters flowed back as they were before. All the Egyptians were drowned. God's people were safe.

Think Spot

The Passover lamb, the blood on the door posts and the miraculous escape of the Israelites remind us of another great escape. Jesus Christ shed his blood for his people so that they would escape eternal death.

Salvation

Page 41

Memory Verse

Stand firm and you will see the deliverance the Lord will bring you today (Exodus 14:13).

Bible Explorer

In the Wilderness

Moses and the Israelites had many adventures on their journey. God looked after them. God led the Israelites on their journey by a pillar of cloud by day and a pillar of fire by night. After a few weeks the people began to complain. There was not much to eat and they longed for the food they had in Egypt.

Water from the Rock

When the Israelites had no water and were thirsty they complained again. Moses cried out to the Lord for help. "Take your rod," God told Moses, "and strike the rock. Water will come out of it." Moses did as God said and there was plenty of water for the people to drink.

Manna

Page 44

God provided for them too. He sent small birds, called quails, for them to eat and in the morning the ground was covered with a white substance called "Manna" - bread sent from heaven by God. Each family had to gather enough for themselves for one day. Any left over would rot. But on the sixth day they had to gather twice as much, enough for the Sabbath day too, and miraculously that portion did not get spoiled. For forty years God provided this food for his people until they had settled in the land he had promised.

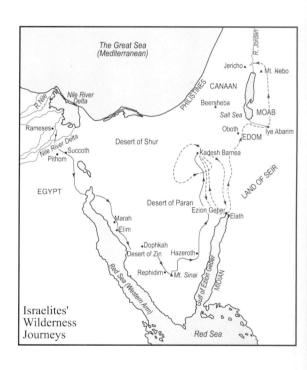

Israelites' Wilderness Journeys

Fact File

Jesus and Manna: Jesus spoke about the Israelites eating the manna in the wilderness.
Page 125

A Quail: A small brown bird. A member of the partridge family.

Page 46

Page 43

Battle with the Amalekites

The Amalekites came to fight against the Israelites. Moses told Joshua to take some men to fight against them. Moses stood on top of a near-by hill to watch. When he raised up his hands the Israelites started winning, but if he let his hands down, the other side did better. As he raised his arms he was praying to God for the Israelite soldiers. Moses' arms became so tired that he found it hard to keep them up all the time. Aaron, his brother and Hur sat Moses down on a rock and they held up his hands and supported him. So Joshua and his men defeated the Amalekites.

 Think Spot

The Israelites complained a lot instead of thanking God for his goodness. Think now of one thing you would like to thank God for. You could thank God for the wonderful gift of his son Jesus Christ who died on the cross to save his people from their sins.

Salvation ☒

Page 43

 Memory Verse

But he brought his people out like a flock; he led them like sheep through the desert (Psalm 78:52).

Bible Explorer

Mount Sinai

When the Israelites reached Sinai God told them, "If you obey me and keep my covenant you shall be a special treasure to me, a kingdom of priests and a holy nation." The people promised faithfully to obey God. They then gathered at the foot of Mount Sinai for three days. No one

Page 43

was allowed to touch God's holy mountain. The mountain shook and was covered in smoke. There was thunder and lightning. A trumpet sounded loudly and the people were afraid. God was there. He called Moses up the mountain, alone at first, then again with Aaron.

God gave Moses detailed laws explaining how to work out the commandments in daily living. These were about how to worship God, how to stay healthy, how to live in the family and community. Moses wrote them down. He was on Mount Sinai receiving God's laws for forty days and forty nights. Then God gave him two tablets of stone with the ten commandments written on them by the finger of God.

The Ten Commandments

God told Moses all his commands for his people. Look up the Explorer Icons to read more about some of these commandments.

1. You shall not worship any other God but me.
Page 94

2. You shall not make any idol.
Page 72

3. You shall not speak God's name in vain.

4. Keep the Sabbath day holy.
Page 14

5. Honour your father and mother.
Page 86

6. You shall not murder.
Page 17

7. You shall not commit adultery.
Page 68

8. You shall not steal.
Page 54

9. You shall not bear false witness.

10. You shall not covet what belongs to someone else.

1. You shall not worship any other God but me.

2. You shall not make any idol.

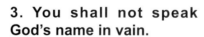

3. You shall not speak God's name in vain.

4. Keep the Sabbath day holy.

5. Honour your father and mother.

6. You shall not murder.

7. You shall not commit adultery.

8. You shall not steal.

9. You shall not bear false witness.

10. You shall not covet what belongs to someone else.

The Golden Calf

The Israelite people did not take long to break their covenant with God. They grew impatient waiting for Moses to come down from Mount Sinai. "Make us an idol to worship," they said to Aaron. He gathered earrings from all the people and melted them to make a model calf, which they worshipped and to which they made sacrifices.

When Moses came down the mountain and saw the idol and the people dancing around, he became very angry. He threw the two tablets of stone to the ground breaking them in pieces. He ground the golden calf to powder, mixed it with water and made the people drink it. Moses prayed to the Lord, begging for forgiveness for the sin of the people.

Page 51

Page 47

Fact File

The Ten Commandments: Jesus summed up the ten comandments like this: "Love the Lord your God with all your heart and with all your soul and with all your mind and with all your strength ... Love your neighbour as yourself." Mark 12: 30-31.

Think Spot

Do you find the commandments difficult to keep? Jesus is the only person who ever kept the commandments perfectly, yet he had to suffer to give his people freedom, hope and eternal life.

Salvation
X
Page 44

Memory Verse

I am the Lord who makes you holy (Exodus 31:13).

Regulations for Worship in the Tabernacle

The name Leviticus refers to "Levites" who were named after Levi, one of Jacob's sons. The Levites were the priests who were in charge of worship. The important message of

Page 46

Leviticus is how to lead a holy life. The people of Israel were told by God how to worship him. Sacrifices of specially chosen animals were to be made on an altar as a way of saying thank-you to God or sorry for the sins committed. These sacrifices were called the: Burnt Offering,

Salvation

Fact File

Grain Offering, Peace Offering, Sin Offering and Trespass Offering. These offerings were given to God by his people until the Lord Jesus Christ made the perfect offering for sin on the cross *once*. The other offerings are now no longer needed.

Feast Days

God told the people to have joyful times of thanksgiving to God along with offering sacrifices for the forgiveness of sin. These feast days were called holy days – that is how we have the word holiday. One of these holy days was the Sabbath – the day of rest every week. Others occured once a year.

Fact File

High Priest: Mediates or acts as a go-between between God and man. He also points to Jesus the great High Priest who made the one sacrifice to pay for sins on the cross.

Salvation

Page 47

Leviticus: This book is the third book of Moses

The Priest

The priest was very important. Aaron, Moses' brother, was the first priest appointed by God. The High Priest had special clothes – a tunic with a sash breastplate, an ephod (a vest with shoulder straps), a robe and a turban. Only he could enter into the Holy of Holies in the tabernacle (or meeting tent) once every year to offer a special sacrifice to God.

The Law

Many detailed laws were given to the people about what food to eat and which things were forbidden. How to treat family and neighbours was also important. One example is "When you reap your harvest leave the grain in the corners and the small amounts that drop in the field. Allow the poor people to gather them up," (Leviticus 19:9–10).

Page 60 & 61

Think Spot

Jesus used the memory verse on this page to explain part of God's law. Think about how different life would be if people followed this law instead of being selfish and putting themselves first.

Memory Verse

Love your neighbour as yourself (Leviticus 19:18).

The Census

God told Moses to take a census of the people to count them or number them. This is why this book is called Numbers.

The children of Israel stayed in the wilderness in different camps for forty years. They sheltered in tents which they carried round with them on their journeys setting up camp in each new place. They would then take these tents down when it was time to move on. This is what we refer to now as a nomadic life or existence. There are still people and cultures today that practice this style of living.

All the time that the Israelites were living in the wilderness the Lord led them with a pillar of fire by night and a pillar of cloud by day. When God's pillar stood still the Israelites remained in their campsite. When the pillar moved, they set off again on their travels following the pillar to the next place.

God guided them and provided for them, but often the people complained and murmured. They were missing the fruit and vegetables and meat they used to get in Egypt. God had provided manna, but they were tired of it.

Fact File

Numbers: This book is the fourth book of Moses.

Quail: These are small brown birds. They are also mentioned in the Book of Exodus.

Page 40

Page 47

Page 56

God was angry with their ingratitude and complaining. Moses prayed earnestly to God. "I will send meat," said God. "Where will you get enough meat to feed this crowd?" asked Moses. "Is the Lord's power limited? Just see what will happen," replied God.

Page 49

God's provision was to send a flock of birds called quails fluttering all around the camp. The children of Israel caught the quails and ate them but as they were eating them God's anger turned on them and many were struck with the plague (sickness). Those who had yielded to their evil desires died from this plague.

Think Spot

God reminded Moses that his power was not limited. Moses saw God's power in amazing ways during his life. Can you remember some of the things Moses saw? When Jesus Christ conquered death this was an even more amazing example of God's power. You can experience God's power in your own life if you trust and believe in him.

Salvation

Page 49

Memory Verse

Ask and it will be given to you; seek and you will find; knock and the door will be opened to you (Matthew 7:7).

Spies

Moses sent twelve men to spy out the Promised Land. When they returned ten of them had a very discouraging report, "The land is beautiful and prosperous but the people are like giants and the cities have strong walls. We can't defeat them."

Only Joshua and Caleb trusted in God. "Do not rebel against God," they said. "If God is pleased with us, he will bring us into the land and give it to us."

Many of the people rebelled and doubted God's provision. God did not allow these people to see the promised land but Joshua and Caleb, who trusted God, did eventually reach the land of Canaan.

Fact File

Promised Land: The name given by the Israelites to Canaan, the land that God had promised to them.

Serpent: Reptile, sometimes poisonous. Also mentioned in Genesis.

Page 15

The Bronze Serpent

The children of Israel were often complaining and moaning against God and his provisions for them. So God sent fierce serpents to the camp. Many people were bitten and died.

Page 58

"We have sinned against God," the rest confessed to Moses. "Please pray that God would take the snakes away."

So Moses prayed for the people. God said to Moses, "Make a bronze serpent and set it up on a pole. Whenever anyone who has been bitten, looks at this bronze serpent he will live."

We are told in John's gospel how Jesus used this incident, in his teaching. "As Moses lifted up the serpent in the wilderness, even so must the Son of Man *(Jesus)* be lifted up, that whoever believes in him should not perish but have eternal life," (John 3:14, KJV.)

Salvation
Page 51

Think Spot

Obeying God is important. Think about how you can obey God.

Memory Verse

The Lord bless you and keep you; the Lord make his face shine upon you, and be gracious to you; the Lord turn his face towards you, and give you peace (Numbers 6:24-26).

God's Law

In the book of Deuteronomy Moses further explains God's law for the people. He reminds them of the

Page 42

commandments God gave them and tells them that if they obey God, all will go well in their new homeland.

The law was summed up with these words which Jesus quoted to his followers. "You shall love the Lord your God with all your heart, with all your soul and with all your

strength." The people were told to teach the law of God to their children and to discuss God's law at home, sitting in the house or out walking, at bedtime and when they got up. It was very important.

When Moses was 120 years old he gathered the people together to give them an important message.

"The Lord has told me that I will not cross over the Jordan into the promised land of Canaan. Joshua will be your new leader. The Lord God will guide you. Be strong and of good courage."

Fact File

Canaan: This was described as a land flowing with milk and honey. This meant it was prosperous and produced good food.

Blessing: When Moses blessed the people of Israel he was asking God to give them good things.

Deuteronomy: This is the fifth book of Moses.

Before Moses died, God showed him the Promised Land from the top of Mount Nebo. Moses was not permitted to enter the land because he had joined the people in their rebellion against God when they were at Meribah Kadesh.

Moses had angrily struck the rock with his rod twice instead of merely speaking to it as God had ordered. He had failed to take God at his word.

Page 53

This disobedience resulted in Moses being kept out of the land of Canaan.

Moses blessed all the tribes of Israel before he died. "Happy are you, O Israel! Who is like you, a people saved by the Lord!"

Salvation

Think Spot

Think Spot

"Who is like you, a people saved by the Lord!" These were Moses' last words. Those who trust in the Lord Jesus are saved by him. They belong to God's family. Read the memory verse - these are special words meant for God's people.

Salvation

Page 52

Memory Verse

Be strong and courageous. Do not be afraid or terrified because of them; for the Lord your God goes with you; he will never leave you nor forsake you (Deuteronomy 31:6).

Life After Moses

Joshua became the leader of the Israelites after the death of Moses. God encouraged him at the start of his great task with these words, "Be strong and of good courage: do not be afraid, nor be dismayed, for the Lord your God is with you wherever you go."

Salvation

☒

Page 55

What a wonderful promise! God is the same today and promises to be with those who trust in him. The name "Joshua" means "The Lord saves" and is similar in meaning to the name "Jesus."

Rahab

Joshua's job was to lead the people into the promised land of Canaan. He sent two men ahead to spy out the land, especially the city of Jericho. They were spotted, but hid in the house of a woman called Rahab. When the soldiers came to her house to fetch them she hid them on the roof under stalks of flax and then sent the soldiers off to look elsewhere.

"When you come to capture the land," she told the spies, "be kind to me and my family because I was kind to you."

The spies escaped from her house down a scarlet rope from her window on the town wall. "Tie this rope in the window as a sign," she was told. "Then you and your family will be safe." The spies then returned to Joshua with an encouraging report. "The Lord will give us the land."

Fact File

Rahab: She is mentioned in the family tree of the Lord Jesus.

 Page 106

Trumpet: This would have been an instrument made from a rams horn. See the picture on page 53.

Joshua: This is an historical book. It tells of the campaign to win the land of Canaan under the leadership of Joshua.

Page 54

Battle of Jericho

The people of Jericho knew that the Israelites were on the way to conquer the land. They were so afraid, that they closed the city gates and stayed inside.

God told Joshua how he must capture the city. Joshua did exactly as God said and told the people what to do.

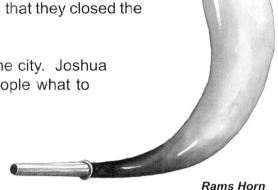
Rams Horn

Battle Plan

Day 1-6
Line up: Soldiers, 7 priests carrying trumpets, then other priests carrying the ark of covenant, then the rest of the soldiers.
Action: All marched round the city.

Day 7
Action: All the people marched round the city of Jericho seven times.
On the seventh time they all shouted.
The walls of Jericho fell down flat.
Joshua and the people conquered the whole city, with God's help.
Rahab and her family were saved.

Think Spot

At what times do you get scared or worried? How would the memory verse on this page help you to cope? Did you know that when Jesus was anxious in the garden of Gethsemane he prayed to God, his father. We should pray when we are worried.

 Page 136

Memory Verse

Be strong and courageous. Do not be terrified; do not be discouraged, for the Lord your God will be with you wherever you go (Joshua 1:9).

Bible Explorer

Achan's Sin

The people were told that all the gold and silver and valuable things in Jericho belonged to God.

Page 42

One man, Achan, stole some silver and gold as well as some clothes and hid them in the ground under his tent. But God saw what he did. Nothing is hidden from him. Achan's wickedness brought a lot of trouble to the people of Israel.

Defeat at Ai

The next city that Joshua wanted to conquer was Ai. The men who were sent out to spy the area thought it would be easy to take this city. What a shock they got when the men of Ai won the battle easily.

Joshua was upset about the defeat. He asked God why it had happened. God told him that someone in the camp had

Page 58

sinned by stealing the precious things which belonged to the Lord. This was why God had allowed their defeat.

Joshua rose early in the morning and followed God's instructions to discover the culprit – Achan.

Joshua confronted Achan with the sin and Achan confessed. The silver and gold and clothes were found buried under his tent. Achan was severely punished. The people threw stones at him until he died. His sin had a terrible result for him.

The Lord God told Joshua to go and capture the city of Ai. This time they were successful. Large numbers of soldiers were placed in hiding on the far side of the city. Joshua and some soldiers attacked the city and then appeared to turn away in defeat.

Fact File

Throwing stones: A Hebrew method of capital punishment. Read Acts 7:54-60 where a godly man, Stephen, was stoned to death because of his love for Jesus Christ. Stephen was the first Christian *martyr* or person put to death for their belief in the Lord Jesus Christ.

Page 144

The men of Ai chased after them leaving the city gates unguarded. The soldiers in hiding walked straight in to Ai and captured it completely. A resounding victory for Joshua and the people of Israel.

After the battle Joshua built an altar to the Lord on Mount Ebal. There the people worshipped the Lord. Joshua read out the whole law of God to the people.

Pages 42 - 45

Joshua led the armies of Israel to many victories. God helped them to win the whole land of Canaan. Then there was peace throughout the land.

The other important task for Joshua was to divide the land of Canaan so that each of the Israelite tribes had its own part to live in.

When Joshua grew old he called the chief men of Israel together and gave them good advice. "You must serve the Lord alone," he urged them. "Choose this day whom you will serve, but as for me and my family, we will serve the Lord." The people replied, "The Lord our God, we will serve and his voice we will obey."

Think Spot

Achan thought he could hide his sin from God. He was wrong. Think about this verse: "You may be sure that your sin will find you out," (Numbers 32:23). When you think of your sin, ask God to forgive you, because of what Jesus Christ has done.

Salvation

Page 57

Memory Verse

We will serve the Lord our God and obey him (Joshua 24:24).

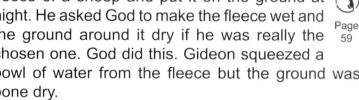

Trouble in Israel

The people of Israel were in trouble. Their enemies from Midian were stealing their crops. The Israelites were frightened and prayed to God.

Next Paragraph

God sent an angel to speak to a man called Gideon who was working at a wine press. The angel said that God had chosen him to save the Israelites, Gideon was surprised and wondered how he would do this.

Gideon made a meal of bread, meat and broth for the angel. The angel told him to put the food on a rock and pour the broth over it. The angel touched the food with the end of his stick and fire gushed out of the rock and burnt up all the food. Then the angel disappeared. Gideon realised he had seen the angel of the Lord so he built an altar and worshipped God. God then told him to destroy the altars of the idol Baal. God was angry with the Israelites because they worshipped this idol. Gideon and his helpers burnt the altars to the ground. To be sure that God had chosen him Gideon asked God for a special sign. He took the

Next Column

fleece of a sheep and put it on the ground at night. He asked God to make the fleece wet and the ground around it dry if he was really the chosen one. God did this. Gideon squeezed a bowl of water from the fleece but the ground was bone dry.

Page 59

Then Gideon asked that the next night the ground would be wet and the fleece dry. When this happened Gideon was certain that he would lead the Israelites to safety. The Midianite and Israelite armies were big. God told Gideon to make his army smaller so that when they won they would not boast about their strength. All who were afraid were sent home. This left 10,000 men. God said it was still too big. So they went to the river. Those who drank water with their hands stayed. Those who put their heads down to the water were sent home. Now there was only 300 men left.

Fact File

Judges: A book containing stories of Israelite national heroes called Judges. It is an historical book that teaches us to follow God.

Winepress: Farmers used this to squeeze out the juice of the grape to make wine.

Gideon prepared for battle. Each soldier had a trumpet and a burning flame which was then covered by an earthenware jar. They all followed Gideon. When he blew his trumpet they all did the same and everyone smashed their jars so that the flames shone brightly. They all shouted loudly "The sword of the Lord and of Gideon."

The Midianites, frightened, started fighting with each other and ran away. God saved the people of Israel using Gideon and a very small army. The people wanted Gideon to be king but he said he wouldn't rule over them. The Lord would be their ruler.

 Think Spot

Gideon was God's special man for this time in the history of the Jews. Gideon cannot help us today but Jesus Christ will help us today. He is the Saviour of the world.

Salvation  Page 59

Memory Verse

The Lord will rule over you (Judges, 8:23).

Samson

The angel of the Lord told Samson's parents they would have a son. Since he would be a Nazirite his hair was not to be cut. He would deliver the Israelites from the Philistines. Samson grew up very strong. Once, on his way

See Below

to see a Philistine woman he wanted to marry, a lion attacked him. With God's help he killed it. He travelled on and Samson talked with

the woman and liked her. When he returned to marry her, he saw that bees had made honey inside the dead lion. He took some for his parents but didn't tell them where it was from. At his wedding Samson told a riddle, "Out of the eater, something to eat; out of the strong something sweet." If the Philistines couldn't solve this riddle in seven days they had to give Samson thirty sets of clothes. But if they did solve it Samson had to give them thirty sets of clothes."

Samson's wife cried until he explained the riddle to her. She then told the others and they won the challenge. Samson was so angry he killed thirty men and took their clothes for the Philistines. His wife then married someone else.

Page 65

Page 64

This made Samson even angrier. He caught 600 foxes, tied them in pairs by their tails, fastened burning torches to them and let them loose in the corn fields. The Philistines were furious. Men from Judah captured Samson but Samson broke loose and killed 1,000 men with a donkey's jawbone. Later he fell in love with a woman called Delilah. The Philistines asked her to discover the secret of his strength. Three times Samson lied to her but he finally told her the truth. If his hair was cut he would become as weak as any man. That night Delilah got a man to shave off Samson's hair. The Philistines captured him, gouged out his eyes and put him in prison.

Fact File

A Riddle: A puzzling question.

Nazirite: A man set apart for God in a special way.

Samson couldn't save himself this time. His strength had gone. But in prison his hair grew again and one day he was brought up to the temple so all could see him and be entertained. Samson stood beside the temple pillars and leant on them. Then he prayed to God for stength so that he could get revenge on the Philistines.

 Page 62

The Lord gave him strength and he pushed the two pillars down, making the temple collapse. Samson died with the Philistines. He killed more people at his death than he had during his life.

 Think Spot

Samson was very strong. God is even stronger. He is stronger than any man. Just think Jesus Christ was the only one strong enough to conquer death. No one else has this power over death!

Salvation

Page 61

 Memory Verse

Be strong in the Lord and in his mighty power (Ephesians 6:10).

Bible Explorer

A Young Woman's Story

There was a famine in Bethlehem. A man called Elimelech took his wife Naomi and sons, Mahlon and Kilion, to Moab so that they could get food to eat. Elimelech's sons married two Moabite women called Ruth and Orpah.

However, tragedy struck the small family and Naomi's husband, Elimilech, died, then his two sons, Mahlon and Kilion, also died. This left, Naomi, Ruth and Orpah as widows with no men to support or provide for them. It was a dreadful situation.

Naomi thought that she should go back to her own people in Bethlehem. Ruth and Orpah followed her even though Naomi kept telling them to go back home. Orpah decided to go back to Moab, but Ruth would not. She said to Naomi, "Where you go I will go and where you stay I will stay. Your people will be my people and your God my God."

Ruth and Naomi arrived in Bethlehem at the harvest time. Ruth wanted to see if she could find some grain to make bread. So she went gleaning in the fields.

Page 45

Fact File

Ruth: The events that take place in this book occur at the end of the age of the Judges. Ruth was one of the ancestors of the Lord Jesus Christ.

Page 106

Gleaning: To gather useful parts of the crop after a field is harvested.

God guided her to a field belonging to Boaz. Boaz came to see how his workers were getting on and noticed Ruth and asked who she was. He found out that she was Naomi's daughter-in-law. Boaz went to speak to Ruth and was very kind to her asking her to always glean in his fields and help herself to water when she was thirsty. Naomi was pleased to hear how well Ruth got on in the fields and how she had met Boaz.

Boaz was a relative of Naomi's husband, Elimelech. By law the closest family relative of Ruth's husband should marry her now that she was a widow. Naomi told Ruth to go to Boaz after work while he was resting and ask him if he would redeem or buy back their family's land.

Page 64

Boaz was delighted to be asked to buy back the land and he was happy to marry Ruth, but there was one relative closer to Naomi's family than he. Boaz had to check that this other family relative was willing for him to take Naomi's land and marry Ruth. As a sign that he was happy for Boaz to redeem the land the other relative took off his shoe and gave it to him.

Boaz became Ruth's redeemer. Jesus Christ is the redeemer of his people. He did this by giving his life so that many sinners could be forgiven. Boaz now married Ruth and they had a son called Obed, whose grandson was King David.

Salvation ☒
Page 63

Think Spot

Ruth chose to follow God and to be with God's people. Would you make the same choice as Ruth? When do you have to make choices about being loyal to God? When you are under pressure to disobey God what is the best way to cope? Pray to God and he will help you.

Memory Verse

May you be richly rewarded by the Lord, the God of Israel, under whose wings you have come to take refuge (Ruth 2:12).

A Young Mother's Story

Elkanah had two wives, Hannah and Peninnah. Peninnah had children, but Hannah had none. Hannah longed to have children and would cry and stop eating because she was so sad. Every year Elkanah and his family went to Shiloh to worship and make sacrifice to the Lord. Hannah was at the temple and she made a vow to God that if he would give her a son then she would give him to the Lord for all the days of his life.

Next paragraph

Eli the priest saw her and thought she was drunk but Hannah explained that she was troubled and pouring out her heart to the Lord. Eli understood and said, "May God grant you what you have asked of him." In time Hannah had a baby boy called Samuel which means, "I asked the Lord for him." When he was a little older she took him to the temple to serve the Lord as she had promised. Hannah thanked God for his provision and power and Samuel grew up to serve the Lord.

Page 63

Fact File

Samuel: He was a Hebrew prophet and judge. The books in the Bible named after him tell of his life and of the two Israelite Kings he anointed - Saul and David.

Vow: a solemn promise.

One night the Lord called Samuel. Samuel thought it was Eli and ran to see what he needed. Eli told him he didn't need anything and to go back to bed. This happened three times and then Eli realised that it was God calling. He told Samuel that if he heard the Lord again to say, "Speak Lord, for your servant is listening." When it happened again Samuel knew what to say and listened.

 Page 68

God said he would judge Eli's family because his sons had sinned. Eli hadn't restrained them when he knew what they were doing. Eli insisted that Samuel must tell him what God had said. So he told him everything. Then one day the Israelites brought the ark of the covenant to a battle to bring them victory against the Philistines. However the Israelites lost the battle, and many were killed. The ark of the covenant which belonged to the tabernacle was captured and Eli's sons died. When Eli heard this sad news he fell off his chair and died.

Page 71

When Samuel grew old, his sons judged Israel but the people were displeased with them and asked for a King. Samuel prayed to God for guidance and the Lord guided Samuel to anoint Saul as king.

Think Spot

God said of Jesus Christ, "This is my son, whom I love. Listen to him!" When you read the Bible you are listening to God just like Samuel. God tells of salvation through Jesus Christ. We should listen to and obey God's word.

Salvation

Page 65

Memory Verse

Do not merely listen to the word ... Do what it says (James 1:22).

Bible Explorer

The Brave Shepherd

David was the youngest son of a large family of eight sons. His father Jesse owned many sheep and David looked after them. David was brave. He rescued a lamb from a fierce lion and even from a huge bear. He was musical too. He played the harp, sang and composed songs called Psalms. Psalm 23 tells of God's love for his people and compares God to a shepherd and his people to sheep. "The Lord is my shepherd: I shall not want. He leads me in green pastures, beside still waters." David's musical skill was later used to soothe King Saul when he was depressed.

Page 66

Page 68

Page 84

Harp

Anointed King

David's life changed dramatically one day. He was called in from looking after the sheep to meet Samuel the priest. God had told Samuel to go to Jesse's house and select one of his sons to be king after Saul, who had displeased God.

Jesse introduced his sons to Samuel, but he turned each one down. "Have you no other sons?" Samuel asked.

"The youngest, David, is looking after the sheep."

Shepherd's Staff

"Fetch him," Samuel ordered. When Samuel saw young David, God told him, "This is the one. Anoint him as king."

All his brothers watched as Samuel anointed David. From that day the Spirit of God was with David in a powerful way.

David Fights Goliath

King Saul's army was at war with the Philistines who had a soldier, Goliath, over three metres tall. Everyone was scared of him. One day Jesse sent David to the army camp to see how his brothers were.

Fact File

Sling and stone: These were used to frighten away wild animals or to direct a straying sheep or lamb back to the flock. **Rod and staff:** These are sticks to pull a lamb from the dangerous place or direct and guide sheep.

Anoint: This means to pour oil on the head or body. A symbol of being set apart for a special task.

David heard Goliath's insults and wondered why no one fought him. Goliath was insulting the army of God's people. David offered to fight Goliath. "God helped me fight a lion and a bear. He will help me fight Goliath," he proclaimed. Saul offered David his heavy armour but David refused it and went to a brook, picked up five smooth stones and put them in his bag. Goliath was angry when he saw David.

Page 66

Shepherd's Sling

David called out, "I fight in the name of the Lord God. He will help me to win."

David then took a stone, slung a shot with his shepherd's sling and struck Goliath in the forehead. Goliath fell down dead. David pulled out Goliath's sword and used it to cut off Goliath's head. The Philistines were shocked. They fled for their lives pursued by Saul's army. David, now a national hero, became a successful, high-ranking soldier.

 Think Spot Do you like someone because they look good or dress well? Read the memory verse. God doesn't look at your skin or clothes. He looks at your heart. Do you love God with all your heart? Do you love him for his gift of salvation?

Salvation

Page 67

Memory Verse

The Lord does not look at the things man looks at. Man looks at the outward appearance, but the Lord looks at the heart (1 Samuel 16:7).

Saul's Jealousy

When the Israelite army returned to Jerusalem David received a hero's welcome. Women danced and sang, "Saul has slain his thousands and David his tens of thousands." This made Saul jealous and angry. **Next Column** David was being given more credit than Saul himself. He was so jealous he even tried to kill David. But God kept him safe. David behaved wisely in all his ways and the Lord was with David.

Michal - Loyal Wife

David married Michal, Saul's daughter. She loved David very much. When her father was plotting against David, she was loyal to her husband. Michal **Page 67** warned David that her father Saul was intending to kill him and let David out through the bedroom window. Michal then put a big pillow in the bed making it look as though David was asleep there. This tricked Saul's men and allowed David time to escape.

Jonathan's Friendship

Jonathan, Saul's son, was a very good friend to David. He was not jealous or resentful like his father. He realised that David was God's choice as the next king and he accepted that willingly.

But Saul was so angry with David that David was forced to flee. Jonathan helped him to escape safely. David hid in the woods wondering whether he ought **Page 67**

to run for his life. Jonathan realised that his father was jealous enough to want to kill David. So David and Jonathan agreed a signal so that Jonathan could tell David if it was safe to return to the palace or not. Jonathan went out to shoot arrows with a servant boy near the place where David was hiding. He shot an arrow away into the distance and called out to his servant, "The arrow is beyond you." This was the secret sign which David heard and so he knew that he had to run away.

David did not repay Saul with evil and hatred. He did not harm him even when he had the opportunity. He respected him as King.

Abigail

When David and his followers were in the wilderness. He sent his men to ask a local farmer, Nabal, if he could give them some food and water, since they had treated his shepherds and flocks with kindness. However, Nabal was a grumpy fellow. "Why should I give my food to you? Who is this David anyway?" he grumbled.

Page 68

David then told his men to put on their swords and get ready to fight. Nabal's wife, Abigail, heard from a servant what Nabal had said to David's soldiers. "They were good to us, protected us and did us no harm." Abigail was wise and quite the opposite to her grumpy selfish husband. She

 immediately prepared
Page
75 loaves, wine, mutton, corn, raisins and figs and took the food to David and his

army. She spoke graciously to him. David's anger disappeared. He was grateful to Abigail for saving him from shedding blood. Shortly after this Nabal took ill and died. David sent for Abigail and she became his wife.

> Think Spot
>
> Friendship is a wonderful thing. What things do you value in a friend? Companionship, a sense of humour, loyalty? Jonathan was a loyal friend to David. In John 15:13 we are told, "Greater love has no-one than this, that he lay down his life for his friends." Jesus **Salvation** Christ is the best friend X ever. He gave up his life for the ungodly. Page 68

 Memory Verse

A friend loves at all times (Proverbs 17:17).

Bible Explorer

David The King

Saul and Jonathan were killed by the Philistines. David became king, captured the city of Jerusalem and made it his capital. But he did not forget his friend Jonathan. "Is there any living of Saul's family? I would like to show them kindness for Jonathan's sake." He was told that Jonathan's son, Mephibosheth, was alive though lame on both feet. David sent for him, "Don't be afraid. I want to give you your family land. Eat with me at my table."

Mephibosheth was amazed at David's generosity and love.

> **King David's generosity should remind us of the generosity and love shown us by the King of Kings, the Lord Jesus Christ.**

David's Sin

One day David stayed at home instead of going to battle. He looked out from his palace roof and noticed a beautiful woman. He found out that she was Bathsheba, the wife of Uriah. David fell in love with her and wanted her for himself. He made devious plans for Uriah, one of his soldiers, to be placed in the fiercest part of the battle. Uriah was killed. After a short time Bathsheba became David's wife. but God was displeased with David.

Nathan

God sent Nathan the prophet to see David. He told David a story. "Two men lived in a city, one rich and one poor. The rich man had lots of animals but the poor man had just one little ewe lamb. When the rich man had visitors, he did not take one of his own flock, but took the poor man's lamb, killed it and cooked it for dinner."

David was angry. "What a terrrible thing to do. He must be punished."

"You are the man," replied Nathan. "You took Uriah's wife."

David realised his sin. He wrote Psalm 51, begging God to forgive him and cleanse him from his sin.

Page 72

Page 80

Page 84

Page 70

Fact File

Jerusalem: This is still a city in Israel today. It has a fascinating and turbulent history. It is here that Jesus Christ was crucified.

Salvation

Page 69

David's sin: This was the sin of adultery. This is against God's law. David broke the seventh commandment.

Page 42

David and Absalom

Unfortunately, Absalom, one of David's sons, caused great grief to his father. He tried to oust David from the throne. However, David still loved his son. Even in the battle between David's men and Absalom and his men, David gave the order, "Deal gently for my sake with the young man, Absalom."

Then one day Absalom was riding in the woods when his long thick hair got caught in the branch of a tree. His mule galloped on and he was trapped. One of David's men, Joab, killed Absalom with three darts. When David heard the news of his son's death, he was greatly distressed, "O Absalom, my son, if only I had died for you."

 Think Spot

David would have willingly died for Absalom but that was not part of God's plan. It was however God's plan that Jesus should give up his life. Jesus willingly gave his life to save those who believe in his name.

Salvation X
Page 71

 Memory Verse

Wash away all my iniquity and cleanse me from my sin (Psalm 51:2).

Page 84

Solomon's Wisdom

Solomon became the King of Israel after his father David died. One day he went to the holy place at Gibeon to offer sacrifices to God. God appeared to him in a dream and said, "Ask me for whatever you want." Solomon's answer pleased God. "Give me an understanding heart so that I will have wisdom to judge your people."

Page 71

God gave Solomon the wisdom he asked for and also riches and honour and the promise of a long life if he obeyed God's laws.

One day Solomon's wisdom was put to the test. Two women came to him both claiming to be the mother of the same baby boy.

One of the woman explained to Solomon, "We live in the same house. I had a baby and this woman had a baby three days later.

This woman's child died in the night and she came and stole my child while I slept and laid her dead child by me."

The other woman denied this, "No, I am the living baby's mother." Solomon said, "Bring me a sword. We will divide the child in two and give you half each." The first woman cried out, "Oh, no, give her the child, please do not kill him."

Solomon knew that she was the real mother and gave the baby back to her. Solomon was wiser than any other man. His fame spread far and wide.

The Temple

In the fourth year of his reign, Solomon began to build the temple. The house of the Lord was about 30 metres long, 10

Fact File

1st and 2nd Kings: These are books that tell the history of the kings of Israel starting with Solomon, and then the many kings of the divided kingdom of Israel and Judah.

metres broad and 15 metres high. It was built of stone already prepared so that there was no sound of hammering or cutting in the temple as it was being built.

The walls and floors and ceilings were made of beautiful cedar wood. The whole house was covered with pure gold, as well as the altar. The whole building inside and out was magnificent. The decoration and furnishings were wonderful. It took seven years to finish all the work.

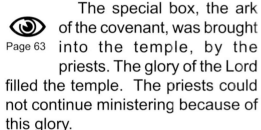
Page 63

The special box, the ark of the covenant, was brought into the temple, by the priests. The glory of the Lord filled the temple. The priests could not continue ministering because of this glory.

Page 72

Solomon blessed all the congregation of Israel, and prayed to the Lord, "O Lord, God of Israel, there is no God like you, in heaven above or on earth below ... Hear from heaven, your dwelling place, and when you hear, forgive," (1 Kings 8:23 & 30).

Queen of Sheba

Solomon's fame spread to other countries too. The Queen of Sheba heard about him and his magnificent wealth and wisdom. She decided to see for herself if the reports were true. "The half was not told me," she declared to Solomon. "Blessed be the Lord your God who favours you and has made you ruler over Israel." They exchanged presents and the Queen of Sheba returned home.

> **The Lord Jesus spoke about the Queen of Sheba's visit to Solomon. When some of the people of his time did not believe his words he said, "The Queen of the South *(i.e. Sheba)* will rise at the day of judgement with this generation and condemn it; for she came from the ends of the earth to listen to Solomon's wisdom and now one greater than Solomon *(i.e. Jesus, the Son of God)* is here,"**
> **(Matthew 12:42).**
>
> **Salvation**
> Page 73

Think Spot

Solomon asked for wisdom from God. What would you have asked for in the same situation? What do you want to ask God for now?

Memory Verse

The fear of the Lord is the beginning of wisdom, and knowledge of the Holy One is understanding (Proverbs 9:10).

Elijah

Elijah loved God. God used him to speak to the people of Israel. One day God told him to tell King Ahab that there would be no rain or dew in Israel for many years. Once Elijah had done this, God said, "Go east across the river Jordan and hide beside the brook Cherith." God made sure Elijah had water from the brook to drink. He even sent ravens with food for him to eat twice a day.

Page 76

Widow of Zarephath

At the city gates a woman was gathering sticks. She was going to prepare a last meal for herself and her son before they died of starvation. Elijah said, "Do not be afraid, cook the meal but first make me a small loaf of bread. Use what is left for yourselves. God has told me your barrel of meal and jug of oil will not run empty until it rains again."

The widow did as Elijah had said and they didn't run out of food. Then one day her son died and she was very distressed.

Elijah took the boy, stretched himself on top of his body three times and prayed. God heard Elijah's prayer and brought the boy back to life. When the widow saw this she knew Elijah was a man of God and that he spoke the truth.

See Below

The Prophets of Baal

Later on King Ahab and Elijah met. Ahab was displeased with Elijah calling him a troublemaker. Elijah said, "I am not a troublemaker. It is you who causes trouble by worshipping Baal instead of God." Elijah then gave a challenge to see which was the true God. Each side would get a bull and lay it on wood. The god who set the wood on fire was the true God. All the prophets of Baal had their turn first. They shouted and danced but there was no answer. Page 42 Elijah made fun of them, "Is Baal busy, or sleeping? Shout louder." The prophets shouted loudly all day but no-one answered.

Elijah then dug a trench round the altar, got men to fill four large jars of water and pour them over the sacrifice - three times. Everything was soaking. Page 75 Elijah prayed to God, "O Lord, prove that you are the true God, and that I am your servant." The Lord sent down fire on the altar, everything was burnt up. When the people saw this they

cried out, "The Lord is God, the Lord is God."
The prophets of Baal were killed. The Lord
proved that he indeed is God.

Elijah then walked for forty days to Mount
Sinai.

Not Alone

He went into a cave to spend the night. God
asked him, "What are you doing here?"

Elijah said, "I am the only one left who
serves the Lord and people are trying to kill
me."

God told him to go to the top of the mountain.
Elijah did this and a fierce wind blew and shattered
the rocks. Then there was an earthquake, then a
fire.

But the Lord didn't use these powerful forces to
speak to Elijah. He spoke in a gentle whisper. When
Elijah heard God's whisper he had to cover his face
with his cloak.

God then told Elijah that there were still 7,000 people
who served him in Israel. He also told him to appoint a man called Elisha to be prophet after
him. When Elijah met Elisha he gave him his cloak as a sign that he was to be his successor.

Think Spot

God encouraged Elijah by speaking to him. He told him that he wasn't alone. We are not alone either. God is always with us. The only person who was ever totally alone was the Lord Jesus Christ as he hung on the cross. "Why have you left me?" he called out to God.

Salvation

Page 74

Memory Verse

The Lord Almighty is with us; the God of Jacob is our fortress (Psalm 46:7).

Elisha

God told Elijah to choose Elisha to succeed him. Elisha agreed. Elijah knew he would soon go to heaven. "What can I do for you, before I am taken away?" he asked Elisha. "Let me have a double share of your spirit," Elisha replied. Elisha wanted double the amount of mighty power that Elijah had. Suddenly a chariot of fire drawn by horses appeared. Elijah was swept into it and carried up to heaven as Elisha looked on.

The Poor Widow

One day a widow came to Elisha for help. "My sons are going to be sold as slaves to pay my debts. All I have is a little oil." Elisha said, "Ask your friends to lend you lots of empty jars and then pour the oil into the jars." The woman did this. Only when all the jars were full did the oil stop. She sold the oil and was able to pay all her debts.

The Shunammite's Son

Elisha travelled a lot. In the town of Shunem he would eat in the house of a rich couple. They prepared a special little room for him. One day Elisha found out that his hostess had no children and her husband was old. He gave her amazing news, "You will have a baby in about a year's time." A year later she gave birth to a son. The boy grew strong and fit until one morning he was in the fields with his father. Suddenly he called out, "My head, my head!"

Fact File

Leprosy: Used in the Bible to describe a number of very infectious skin diseases. It was greatly feared and infected people had to live away from their families and friends.

Think Spot

Naaman was cleansed from his leprosy by washing in the Jordan. God's people are cleansed from sin through the work of the Lord Jesus Christ. "If we confess our sins, God is faithful and just to forgive us our sins and to cleanse us from all unrighteousness," (1 John 1:9, KJV).

Salvation

Page 77

"Carry him home to his mother," his father told a servant. The sick boy sat on his mother's knee until noon and then he died. The heart-broken mother carried him to Elisha's room and laid him on the bed. She then fetched Elisha, insisting that he came to her house.

Page 78

Elisha went into the room and shut the door. He prayed to the Lord. He stretched himself out on top of the boy and soon the boy's body grew warm. Elisha paced up and down the room. Once more he stretched out on top of the boy. This time the boy sneezed seven times and opened his eyes. God had answered Elisha's prayer. How thankful the mother was to have her little boy restored to life.

Page 83

Naaman

Naaman, a wealthy and important leader in the Syrian army, decided to visit Elisha. He had leprosy - a terrible skin disease. A servant girl who had been captured from Samaria suggested that he go to the prophet, Elisha, for a cure. When he arrived Elisha sent out a messenger to tell him to wash in the River Jordan seven times. Naaman was not impressed. "I have far better rivers at home," he argued. However his servants persuaded him to listen to the advice and when Naaman came out of the river for the seventh time his skin was as smooth as a baby's. What a miracle! Naaman was delighted. He went back to Elisha and confessed, "The God of Israel is the only true God."

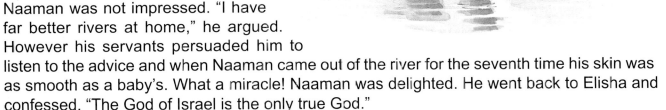

Memory Verse

If you confess with your mouth, 'Jesus is Lord,' and believe in your heart that God raised him from the dead, you will be saved (Romans 10:9).

Kings of Israel and Judah

After Solomon died his son Rehoboam became king. The people rebelled against him because he made them work like slaves. The Israelites in the northern kingdom made Jeroboam king. Only the tribes of Judah and Benjamin in the south remained loyal to the family of David. The kingdom was divided. The kings of the northern kingdom of Israel did not obey God's laws.

Ahab and Jezebel

Ahab was a bad king who married a wicked woman Jezebel. He built altars and a temple for the false god Baal. Elijah warned Ahab about his behaviour.

Joash

Uzziah

However, some kings in the southern kingdom, Judah, were good.

Asa did what was right in God's sight. He removed the altars to false gods and destroyed idols. He ordered the people to obey God and the whole country lived at peace.

Joash was seven years old when he was crowned king. Jehoiada, the priest, masterminded a plan to give Joash his rightful throne in spite of his wicked grandmother. Joash did what was right when guided by Jehoiada but after Jehoiada died, Joash listened to bad advice and turned away from the true God.

Uzziah was sixteen when he became king. He did what was right and God made him prosper. He built towers and fortresses in Jerusalem and in the desert. He dug wells to find water for his animals. He had farms and vineyards which he loved. He became famous but very proud and this led to him going into the temple and performing the duties which only the priests were allowed to do. When the priests challenged him, he was furious. Even the king has to obey God. As a punishment the Lord gave Uzziah the skin disease leprosy. He had to live in isolation till the day of his death.

Page 84

Hezekiah

Hezekiah brought back the true worship of God and ordered the singing of praise to God using the Psalms of David and Asaph. When the King of Assyria came to fight Hezekiah and the people of Judah, Hezekiah encouraged his people, "The Lord God is with us, to help us and to fight our battles." God did indeed deliver them from the enemy.

Pages 84 & 85

Josiah was eight years old when he became king When he was sixteen he committed himself to the ways of God. The temple was repaired under his instructions. The workmen found an old scroll, a lost copy of the law of God. Josiah called everyone together and read God's law out loud. The people promised to keep God's law.

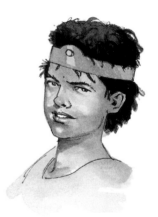

Josiah

Fact File

Babylon and Judah:
The King of Babylon fought against Judah. The people were taken away as captives to live in a foreign land for many years.

1st and 2nd Chronicles:
This covers the same period of time as 1st and 2nd Kings and some of 2nd Samuel.

 **Think Spot**

Israel and Judah had many different kings over the years. Jesus is called the King of Kings and is the ruler who does everything perfectly and lives for ever.

 Memory Verse

The wages of sin is death, but the gift of God is eternal life in Christ Jesus our Lord (Romans 6:23).

Salvation ☒

 Page 79

@ Page 77

Ezra and Nehemiah

Both Ezra and Nehemiah are about the rebuilding of Jerusalem after the people had been captives in Babylon for many years. Cyrus, King of Persia, defeated Babylon and allowed the Jewish people to go back home to Jerusalem.

First a leader called Zerubbabel and a priest called Joshua led a group back to Jerusalem. They began the big task of rebuilding the temple, starting with the altar. They followed the directions given to Moses by God. They sacrificed burnt offerings to the Lord God every morning and evening, asking for forgiveness of sin. When the foundations of the temple were laid some time later the people had a big celebration – shouting, "Praise the Lord."

Next Column

But work was stopped because of opposition from enemies, and was not resumed for many years, until Darius became king of Persia. But the leaders of the Jews were under God's watchful eye and the work was completed.

Ezra

Ezra the priest was sent to Jerusalem by King Artaxerxes to make sure that the people were observing God's law. When he found that the people had not been obeying all God's laws, he prayed earnestly to God confessing the sin and asking for forgiveness and help to put things right.

See Below

Nehemiah

Nehemiah worked for the King Artaxerxes as a wine steward. He had heard from Jerusalem that those building the walls were not getting on well at all. Nehemiah prayed to God confessing his sin and asking for help.

Page 79

When he served the king wine, Artaxerxes noticed that Nehemiah looked sad. "What is troubling you?" he asked. "The city of my family is in ruins and the walls are burned down," Nehemiah replied. "What do you want?" the king asked.

Fact File

Ezra: Tells the story of the return of the Jews from their captivity in Babylon.

Nehemiah: Written like a diary, this book tells about how the walls of Jerusalem were rebuilt.

Next Paragraph

Nehemiah quickly prayed and asked the kings permission to go to Jerusalem to rebuild the walls. The king was willing to let him go.

When Nehemiah arrived in Jerusalem he spent three days surveying the damage. A lot of work had to be done. The people were keen to start. They had a difficult job. The wall had to be built high and wide around the city. They had opposition from Sanballat who said the wall would be useless. Tobiah mocked them too, "If a fox climbed on that wall, it would fall down."

See Below

Nehemiah trusted in God and prayed again for help. God answered Nehemiah's prayer and helped them so much that soon half of the huge wall was finished. Sanballat and his wicked friends made a plot to attack the wall. Nehemiah prayed again and told the builders to carry a sword in one hand and work with the other.

Page 80

With God's help the wall was finished in only fifty two days. Everyone, including children, worshipped God. Ezra stood on a wooden platform and read and explained God's law to them. The people were encouraged by the words, "The joy of the Lord is your strength," (Nehemiah 8:10).

Think Spot

The joy of the Lord is your strength. How do you get this joy? By trusting and believing in the Lord Jesus Christ as your Saviour.

Salvation
[X]
Page 81

Memory Verse

The joy of the Lord is your strength (Nehemiah 8:10)

Bible Explorer

Esther

Esther was a beautiful Jewish girl who lived in the land of Persia, ruled by King Xerxes. An orphan, she was brought up by her cousin, Mordecai. To show off his vast wealth King Xerxes had a feast for the important people in the land. He ordered his Queen, Vashti, to come and let his guests admire her.

Page 90

She refused. The king was very angry and Vashti was punished. Someone else was to take her place as queen. All the beautiful young girls in the land were told to come to the palace. One would be chosen as the new queen. Each girl had a whole year of beauty treatments.

A New Queen

The king was very pleased with Esther and chose her as queen but Mordecai told her not to tell anyone she was a Jew. Some people did not like the Jewish people. Then one day

Mordecai heard two men plotting to kill the king. Mordecai told Esther who warned King Xerxes. The men were hung and the incident recorded in the royal books.

Haman, a nobleman to whom the king had given a high position, was angry when Mordecai refused to bow down to him. He made the king agree to pass a law that would have all the Jews in Persia killed on a certain day. Esther heard that Mordecai was greatly troubled and sent a servant to find out what was wrong. Mordecai told Esther the situation and asked her to help save the Jews. But Esther knew that anyone who went to see the king, uninvited, was killed unless he put out his golden sceptre. However, Esther decided to try so Mordecai and all the Jews fasted for three days before she went to see the King. When the King saw

Page 82

her he was pleased with her and offered her anything she would like.

Fact File

Esther: A book in the Bible where God's name is not mentioned once but we see him working in the lives of his people.

Memory Verse

You are a shield around me, O Lord (Psalm 3:3).

The Banquet

Esther requested that King Xerxes and Haman come to a banquet with her. They accepted. At the banquet she didn't say anything about the Jews but asked the king and Haman to come again the next day. Haman thought that the king and queen must really like him. But he was still annoyed that Mordecai did not bow to him. Haman's family told him to hang Mordecai on the gallows.

Honour for Mordecai

One night, to help the king sleep, the royal books were read to him. The part where Mordecai saved the king was read out. The king found out that nothing had been done to honour Mordecai so he asked Haman, "What should be done for the man the king delights to honour?" Haman, thought he was the favoured one, and suggested the man should wear royal robes, and a crown and be led through the city on a horse. The king said, "Give that honour to Mordecai the Jew." Haman was horrified to have to honour Mordecai in this way.

Esther Saves the Jews

Haman was then called to Esther's second banquet. The king asked Esther again what she would like. This time she explained and pleaded that her life and the lives of her people the Jews would be spared from Haman's plot. The king was very angry with Haman thinking that he was trying to kill the queen. King Xerxes ordered that Haman should be hung on the gallows he built for Mordecai. Haman was killed and his land and property were given to Esther. Mordecai was made manager of the estate. Esther begged the king to put an end to the evil plan of Haman. So the king passed an edict allowing the Jews the right to defend themselves when attacked. Mordecai was honoured by the king. God worked through Mordecai and Esther to save the Jews from death.

Mordecai

Think Spot

Esther is a Jewish heroine and was used by God to save her people from death. Jesus died on the cross to save us from eternal death. Esther was a rich queen in a comfortable palace. Jesus Christ had to suffer and die to save us.

Salvation

Page 82

Job

Job lived in the land of Uz. He had seven sons, three daughters, 7,000 sheep, 3,000 camels, 500 pairs of oxen, 500 donkeys and a large house. Job's children had homes too and often ate together in one of their houses. Job offered burnt sacrifices to God for them, asking God to forgive their sins.

See Below

Satan's Attacks

God was pleased with how Job respected him and avoided evil. But Satan said, "Job is only good because he has an easy life and plenty possessions. Take that away and he would curse you."

So God allowed Satan to test Job's faith by attacking his possessions. Messengers came to tell Job, "The oxen were ploughing, the donkeys grazing beside them, when robbers came and took them away."

"Fire fell from heaven and burnt up all your sheep."

"Chaldean raiders have taken all your camels."

Then came the greatest blow of all. "Your children were in their oldest brother's house. A great wind struck the house. It fell on them. They are all dead." Job was full of grief at this news but he worshipped God. "The Lord gave and the Lord has taken away. Blessed be the name of the Lord."

Page 83

Satan again challenged God, "Job would not be so faithful if his body was suffering," he said. So God allowed Satan to do what he wanted to Job but his life was to be spared. So poor Job had painful boils all over his body. He was miserable. He sat in a pile of ashes, scraping his sores with a piece of broken pottery. Even his wife urged him to curse God and die. Job refused. "Don't speak so foolishly," he said. "We accept good from God, should we not also accept hardship."

Job's Comforters

Job's three friends, Eliphaz, Bildad and Zophar, came to comfort him. They sat with Job for seven days and nights without saying a word. They were not much comfort to Job. They did not understand what had happened. One urged Job to repent, another accused him of opposing God and that he deserved his suffering. Job responded to his friends in a wise and godly way. He trusted in God through all his suffering. "I know that my Redeemer lives," he said.

Salvation

See Page 84

 Memory Verse

I know that my Redeemer lives (Job 19:25).

Job Restored

Another man, Elihu, gave his opinions on Job's problems. He was not helpful either. Only when God spoke did Job get a right understanding of God's power. He repented for his sinful thoughts and words. Job prayed for his friends too and then God restored all his losses – in fact God gave him twice as much as he had. The Lord blessed Job greatly. He had seven more sons and three beautiful daughters. Job was a patient man, and trusted in God who is very kind and merciful.

Page 90

Page 104

Fact File

 Think Spot

Job's problems were resolved after he prayed for his friends. Remember to pray for your friends, even the ones who may be causing you trouble.

They have the patience of Job: This is someone who is patient like Job was when he faced his problems.

Job's Comforters: People who think they give comfort but in fact make the sufferer feel worse.

Job: The story of a man named Job, his trials and his trust in God.

@ Page 83

Psalm 23

Page 64

Page 86

David was a shepherd in his youth. He composed a psalm that spoke of God as a caring shepherd, and his people as his sheep. "The Lord is my shepherd, I shall not be in want. He makes me lie down in green pastures, he leads me beside quiet waters, he restores my soul. He guides me in the paths of righteousness for his name's sake."

Psalm 117

The shortest psalm is 117. It has only two verses. It is a shout of praise to the Lord for his kindness and truth.

Psalm 119

This is the longest psalm with 176 verses and twenty two parts - one for each letter of the Hebrew alphabet. In the original language each verse of part one begins with the first letter of the alphabet; each verse of part two begins with the second letter and so on through all twenty two parts. The psalm tells how wonderful God's word is. In almost every verse the Psalmist speaks about God's word in different ways - law, testimonies, word, statutes, commandments, precepts and judgements. "Your word is a lamp to my feet and a light for my path," he says in verse 105. It is a sure guide even in darkness or difficulty.

Psalm 51

David wrote Psalm 51 to express his sorrow for sin. He had committed adultery with Bathsheba and had her husband killed. Nathan the prophet confronted David with his sin and David repented. "I have sinned against you," he said to God. "Wash me and I shall be whiter than snow." David begged for forgiveness and mercy.

Page 68

Salvation

Page 87

Jesus and the Psalms

Page 138

Jesus quoted from the Psalms when he was on the cross. He said the words of Psalm 22, "My God, my God, why have you left me."

P

Fulfillment on pages 138 & 139

Many Psalms were fulfilled in the life of the Lord Jesus Christ - even that his hands and feet would be pierced at the crucifixion (Psalm 22), but none of his bones would be broken (Psalm 34).

Psalm 150

This psalm tells of praising God with musical instruments - trumpet, lyre, harp, timbrel (like a tambourine), stringed instruments and flutes and loud clashing cymbals.

Psalm 91

This psalm helps us to trust in God when we are in danger. God is like a safe fortress. With God on our side there is no need to be afraid. When we call on him he will answer. He will be with us in trouble.

Fact File

Psalms: A book of praises. The hymn book that Jesus used. Many psalms are written by David, but also by others like Moses (Psalm 90), Solomon (Psalm 72) and Asaph. There are 150 psalms in the book of Psalms.

Psalm 121

Try reading this psalm when you are going on a long journey or facing a

new situation. "I lift up my eyes to the hills - where does my help come from? My help comes only from the Lord God. He keeps me from danger and from evil, always."

It is good to sing psalms when we are happy - Psalm 100 tells us to "make a joyful shout to the Lord."

It is good for us to sing psalms when we are troubled. Psalm 46 tells us that "God is our refuge and our strength, a very present help in trouble."

Think Spot

There is a psalm to help in every situation. Psalms give comfort when you are sad and help you to praise when you are happy.

 Memory Verse

Is any one of you in trouble? He should pray. Is anyone happy? Let him sing songs of praise (James 5:13).

Bible Explorer

Proverbs

This book has good advice from the wise King Solomon and others. It deals with the importance of **wisdom**. To make the right choices in life you need wisdom. If you are truly wise you will have a right relationship with God: "The fear of the Lord is the beginning of wisdom," 1:7 (KJV); "Trust in the Lord with all your heart and lean not on your own understanding. In all your ways acknowledge him and he shall direct your paths," 3:5-6 (KJV).

Page 42

Good advice is given to **young people**: "Listen, to your father's instruction and do not forsake your mother's teaching," 1:8; "If sinners entice you do not give in to them," 1:10; "Whoever loves discipline loves knowledge but he who hates correction is stupid," 12:1.

We are told how to treat **the poor**: "Do not withhold good from those to whom it is due when it is in your power to act," 3:27; "He who mocks the poor shows contempt for their Maker; whoever gloats over disaster will not go unpunished," 17:5.

Page 91

We are told about how to look after **animals**: "A righteous man cares for the needs of his animal, but the kindest acts of the wicked are cruel," 12:10.

Real values are shown to be more important than wealth: "Better a little with the fear of the Lord than great wealth with turmoil," 15:16.

"A righteous man cares for the needs of his animal...

... but the kindest acts of the wicked are cruel," (Proverbs 12:10).

"Whoever loves discipline loves knowledge...

... but he who hates correction is stupid," (Proverbs 12:1).

We are told seven things that God hates. We must avoid:

*A proud look
*A lying tongue
*Hands that shed innocent blood
*A heart that devises wicked plans
*Feet that are swift in running to evil
*A false witness who speaks lies
*One who sows discord among brothers.

Ecclesiastes

These are words from someone who is referred to as "The Teacher". He looks at life and says that everything is vanity or useless. All human wisdom, achievement, power, wealth or pleasure are vanity. His advice to young people was – "Remember your Creator in the days of your youth," 12:1. He also states that the whole duty of man is to "Fear God and keep his commandments," 12:13.

Song of Solomon

This book is a love song. It expresses the love of the bridegroom and his bride in poetic and beautiful language. The bridegroom speaks endearingly to his beloved as my darling, my dove, my flawless one. The love of husband and wife is a beautiful gift from God. The love of the Lord Jesus Christ for his bride, the church, is much more wonderful.

Salvation [X]
Think Spot

Think Spot — There are many types of love. There is a love between a husband and a wife, between a parent and a child, between friends. All are precious gifts from God. But the most wonderful love is God's love for us. This is the love that Jesus showed when he died on the cross for his people. His love is perfect love. **Salvation** [X]

Page 88

Fact File

Proverbs: Wise sayings mostly by Solomon.
Ecclesiastes: Written by a man called 'The Teacher'.
Song of Solomon: A love song from a bridegroom and a bride.

Memory Verse

Remember your Creator in the days of your youth (Ecclesiastes 12:1).

Isaiah

Salvation
☒
See below

Isaiah points to the coming Messiah. He foretells his birth: "To us a child is born, to us a son is given and the government will be on his shoulders. He will be called 'Wonderful Counsellor, Mighty God, Everlasting Father, Prince of Peace,'" Isaiah 9:6

Ⓟ
Fulfillment on Page 118

He foretells the life of the Messiah. Jesus quotes Isaiah at the start of his ministry, "The Spirit of the Lord is on me because he has anointed me to preach good news to the poor. He has sent me to proclaim freedom for the prisoners and recovery of sight for the blind, to release the oppressed, to proclaim that the time has come when the Lord will save his people," (Isaiah 61:1–2; Luke 4:18–19). Jesus did that – he healed the sick, preached good news and released people from the captivity of sin and Satan.

Isaiah

👁 Page 140

Ⓟ
Fulfillment on Page 138

The death of Jesus is also detailed by Isaiah long before it actually happened. His suffering, pain and rejection are all told by Isaiah. He explains that his death was a sacrifice to bring forgiveness and that for his sake, sinners would be forgiven. (Isaiah 53.)

Salvation
☒
Page 89

Jeremiah

This book is about Jeremiah. He preached God's message faithfully warning the people of Judah against sin and idolatry. He had a hard life. His message was not well received. King Jehoiakim even cut up Jeremiah's prophecies and burned them in a fire. Jeremiah just had them all rewritten. He could not stop speaking God's word so the officials threw him into a muddy pit. Ebedmelech from Ethiopia came to his rescue. He gave Jeremiah old rags to put under his arms and then hauled him up with ropes.

Jeremiah's predictions of disaster came true in his lifetime. Nebuchadnezzar of Babylon defeated Jerusalem, the Temple was destroyed and the king and many people taken captive. But Jeremiah gave a message of hope - God would bring them back home to live in peace.

Lamentations

During this time of destruction and exile Jeremiah wrote the book of Lamentations. Each chapter is a poem. Even in suffering Jeremiah can say that God is good – his love and mercy continue every day. (Lamentations 3:22.) The Lord is good to all who trust in him.

Ezekiel

While the people were in exile in Babylon the prophet Ezekiel gave them God's message. He wanted them to remember that God was with them in Babylon too. Ezekiel saw many strange visions. These were illustrations of the message that God wanted the people to know. In one vision Ezekiel saw a valley of dried bones. The bones then started to move, then join together. Flesh and hair grew on them and the dry bones became people. At first they were lifeless then God commanded them to breathe and they stood up alive. This story gave the people hope that God would bring them back again to their own land.

Jeremiah

Think Spot

Jeremiah was unpopular with the people because he told them that God wanted them to stop sinning. God still tells us this today. If we trust in Jesus Christ he will forgive us. We can ask God for help to conquer sin.

Salvation

Page
91

Memory Verse

The Lord is good to those whose hope is in him, to the one who seeks him (Lamentations 3:25).

Fact File

Vision: A sight given by God for a special purpose.

Major Prophets: The prophets were men who gave the people messages from God. The longer books are called major prophets. They are Isaiah, Jeremiah, Lamentations (also written by Jeremiah), Ezekiel and Daniel.

Daniel

Daniel was a young man from the land of Judah who was captured by King Nebuchadnezzar of Babylon along with many others. Daniel and his three friends were chosen to work in the royal palace. They were taught the new language and had to read many books. Daniel and his three friends loved God and served him.

The King's Dream

One night Nebuchadnezzar had a bad dream. He called his wise men and magicians to see if they could explain it. When they failed the king was angry and wanted to kill them. Daniel then came and asked the king to give him time to interpret the dream. Daniel and his friends prayed to God for help. God helped Daniel understand the dream and when he explained it to the king, the king honoured Daniel by saying, "Surely your God is the God of god's and Lord of kings." Daniel and his friends were promoted to high positions in the land.

Page 91

The King's Feast

After Nebuchadnezzar died Belshazzar became king. During a feast with his nobles a strange thing happened. The finger of a human hand appeared and wrote on the wall. Belshazzar was scared and called on his wise men to explain what this meant. They had no idea.

The queen told Belshazzar not to worry because a man called Daniel could tell him what the writing meant. Daniel was called. The words on the wall were: MENE, MENE, TEKEL, PARSIN and they meant: "Your reign will soon be at an end. You fall short of God's standards. Your kingdom will be conquered and given to someone else."

A Wicked Plot

Daniel was honoured and made third highest in the land but that very night Belshazzar was killed and Darius from Media became king. King Darius wanted to promote Daniel to chief administrator. The other officials were jealous of him and wanted to find fault with him. But they realised Page 95 that Daniel was so honest that they would not catch him out unless it was something to do with worshipping God. So they suggested to King Darius that he make a law stating that anyone who prayed to any god or man except the king in the next thirty days should be put in the lions' den. The king agreed to it.

The Lions' Den

Page 94

Page 95

Daniel knew he could not obey it. He thanked God for his goodness and asked him for help. The officals saw this and reported it. Daniel was put in the lions' den. Beforehand the king said to Daniel, "May your God, whom you always serve, rescue you." That night King Darius was miserable. He couldn't eat or sleep. As soon as it was light he hurried to the lions' den and called out to Daniel, "Has your God been able to save you from the lions?" He was delighted to hear Daniel's reply, "My God sent his angel to shut the lions' mouths. They have not hurt me."

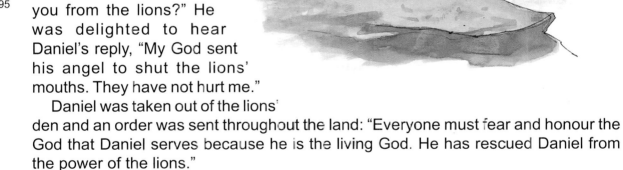

   Daniel was taken out of the lions' den and an order was sent throughout the land: "Everyone must fear and honour the God that Daniel serves because he is the living God. He has rescued Daniel from the power of the lions."

 Memory Verse

But the saints of the Most High will receive the kingdom and will possess it for ever – yes for ever and ever (Daniel 7:18).

 Think Spot

The memory verse mentions the word 'saints'. They are the people of God. If you believe in Jesus Christ you are part of God's kingdom for ever.

Salvation

Page 92

The Minor Prophets

Hosea
Hosea tells us of God's love for his people even in rebellion. There is one verse in Hosea that you should say to God for yourself, "Forgive all our sins and receive us graciously," 14:2.

Joel

Salvation

See below

Salvation

Next Column

Joel speaks of God's punishment and restoration. "Return to the Lord your God for he is gracious and compassionate; slow to anger and abounding in love," 2:13. The lovely promise is given, "Everyone who calls on the name of the Lord will be saved," 2:32.

Amos
Amos, a farmer, warned of God's punishment of sins. He urged the people to "Seek the Lord and live," 5:6.

Obadiah
Obadiah tells how God the Lord will rule the earth. All will be under his power.

Jonah

Page 94 & 95

Jonah's story is about rebellion against God and an amazing adventure at sea!

Bethlehem today

Micah
In Micah 5:2 we are told of God's plan for the world, of God's promise of the Saviour to be born in the little town of Bethlehem. We also hear of the coming Messiah: "Who is a God like you who pardons sin and forgives the transgressions of the remnant of his inheritance. You delight to show mercy," 7:18.

P
Fulfillment on page 106

Nahum
Nahum tells of God's strength and power. "The Lord is slow to anger and great in power," 1:3.

Habakkuk
Habukkuk tells us that we must trust God. "The earth will be filled with the knowledge of the glory of the Lord as the waters cover the sea," 2:14; "In wrath remember mercy," 3:2.

Salvation

Next Paragraph

Zephaniah
Zephaniah warns us that God will judge the world. But hope was offered to God's people in Zion. "The Lord your God is with you he is mighty to save," 3:17.

Salvation

Think Spot

Haggai
Haggai tells of the call to rebuild the house of the Lord – the temple. "You spend money on yourselves and your own homes," said God. "You should be building my house instead of leaving it as a ruin." 1:9

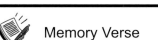
Memory Verse

And everyone who calls on the name of the Lord will be saved (Joel 2:32).

Think Spot

Sometimes the prophets brought messages from God that were gloomy and sad. Many times they gave messages of hope pointing towards God's forgiveness, as in the memory verse.

Salvation

Page 93

Zechariah

Zechariah points to the coming King, "See; your king comes to you, righteous and having salvation, gentle and riding on a donkey, on a colt, the foal of a donkey," 9:9. This was fulfilled when Jesus rode into Jerusalem on a donkey.

P

Fulfillment on page 132

Malachi

In this book we get a message of blessing and hope. "I have loved you," God says. 1:2. "Those who feared the Lord talked with each other and the Lord listened and heard," 3:16. "They will be mine in the day when I make up my jewels," 3:17, KJV.

Salvation

Page 95

Zechariah

Micah tells of God's plan for the world. He tells of God's promise of the Saviour to be born in the little town of Bethlehem. Micah 5:2.

Fact File

Minor Prophets: The last twelve books of the Old Testament - Hosea, Joel, Amos, Obadiah, Jonah, Micah, Nahum, Habakkuk, Zephaniah, Haggai, Zechariah, Malachi. These are called the minor prophets as they are shorter than the major prophetic books. Each has an important message. There are severe warnings against sin and the Saviour Jesus Christ is promised.

Jonah's Disobedience

God told Jonah, "Go to the city of Nineveh. Tell the people that I see their wickedness." Although Jonah loved God, he did not obey him then. He went to Joppa instead. There he got on a boat for Tarshish. He thought he had escaped but God sent a violent storm.

Page 42

The ship was in danger and the sailors were scared. They threw cargo overboard to lighten the ship and prayed to false gods who could not hear them. Jonah slept through the storm until the captain woke him. "Get up and pray to your God. Perhaps he will save us." Then they drew lots to decide who was to blame for the disaster. The blame fell on Jonah. When they discovered that Jonah was running away from God, they were even more afraid.

Drastic Action

Jonah came up with a drastic solution. "Throw me overboard. Then the sea will be calm. It is my fault." The sailors didn't want to do this. They rowed harder but with no success. In desperation they cried out in prayer to God, "O, Lord, please do not let us die because of this man Jonah. Do not blame us. You, O Lord, have done just what pleases you."

Page 95

Fact File

Lots: In Bible times decisions were sometimes made by drawing straws or tossing a coin. The Bible tells us that God was in charge of how that worked out.

Then they caught Jonah and threw him into the raging sea. As soon as he hit the water, the sea became calm. The sailors saw God's power over the wind and

Next Column

sea and worshipped him. But that was not the end of Jonah. God had prepared a great fish to come and swallow him – so saving him from drowning. For three days and

Page 104

nights Jonah lived inside the big fish. In his trouble he cried out to God. "I cried to God because of

Salvation

X
Next Column

my trouble and he heard me. When my soul was fainting I remembered the Lord. I prayed to you. Salvation comes from the Lord."

Jonah's Obedience

Jonah worshipped God, confessed his sin and thanked God for saving him. God made the fish vomit him on to dry land. Jonah had a second chance to obey God's call to go to Nineveh and preach to the people. When he entered Nineveh he walked towards the centre. His message was clear. "In forty days Nineveh will be destroyed because of sin."

The people heard this and repented of their evil doing. They were so sorry for what they had done. The king told everyone, "We must all cry to God, and turn from evil ways. Perhaps God will not destroy us." God had mercy and did not destroy the city. Many people were changed and served God.

Salvation

X
Memory Verse

Jonah's Anger

But Jonah was angry because the destruction did not happen. God taught Jonah another lesson. Jonah watched Nineveh from up on a hill. God caused a plant with big leaves to grow to give Jonah shade. Then God sent a worm to gnaw the plant's roots so that it died. When a hot east wind came Jonah became hotter and more upset. "You are sorry for the plant that has been destroyed," said God. "Should you not have as much pity for the great city of Nineveh?" Jonah himself had been shown mercy. He should have rejoiced that God showed mercy to the people in Nineveh.

Page 108

Page 106

> **The Lord Jesus compares himself to Jonah. As Jonah was three days and three nights inside the huge fish, so Jesus was three days and three nights in the grave.**
>
> Pages 138 – 141

Memory Verse

Salvation comes from the Lord
(Jonah 2:9).

Salvation
X
Page 105

Think Spot

The people cf Nineveh listened to Jonah and repented. They turned from their evil ways to obey God. Can you think of ways in which you should repent and obey God?

Linking Old and New Testaments

The Bible is divided into two sections – the Old Testament and the New Testament. The Old Testament points to the coming of the Messiah or Saviour of the world, the Lord Jesus Christ. The New Testament tells of the Saviour's birth, life and death and explains God's plan of salvation and our responsibility.

The Old Testament and the New Testament are one book. The Old Testament announces beforehand much of what takes place in the New. The New Testament shows us that God's promises to people like Abraham and the prophets have been fulfilled. The New Testament begins with four books called the Gospels. The word Gospel means "Good News."

Four different men - Matthew, Mark, Luke and John - were inspired by God to write their version of the Good News about Jesus Christ. Each gospel is written from a slightly different point of view, emphasising different aspects of Jesus' life and aimed at a different audience. Taken together they give a complete picture of Jesus of Nazareth, both God and man.

Matthew	First written to the Jews. Asks the question: Who was Jesus? *Theme: Jesus as King and Messiah.*
Mark	Written first with non-Jewish people in mind. Asks the question: What did Jesus do? *Theme: Jesus as Servant.*
Luke	Written first to the Greek people. Asks the question: What was Jesus like? *Theme: Jesus as Son of Man.*
John	Written for the Christian World. Asks the question: Why did Jesus come? *Theme: Jesus as Son of God.*

The Gospels do not tell us all about Jesus' life. Only Matthew and Luke tell of his birth. Little is told of the first 30 years of his life. Much of the focus is on the last week of his life. The important central theme of the Bible, Old and New Testaments, is the Lord Jesus Christ, the Son of God, coming to the world as a human in order to save his people from their sins.

John wrote his Gospel "that you may believe that Jesus is the Christ, the Son of God, and that by believing you may have life in his name," John 20:31.

The Bible is God's word. He has recorded it carefully for us and wants us to read it and to study it. When you read the Bible, ask God to help you to understand it and he will.

Map of Israel

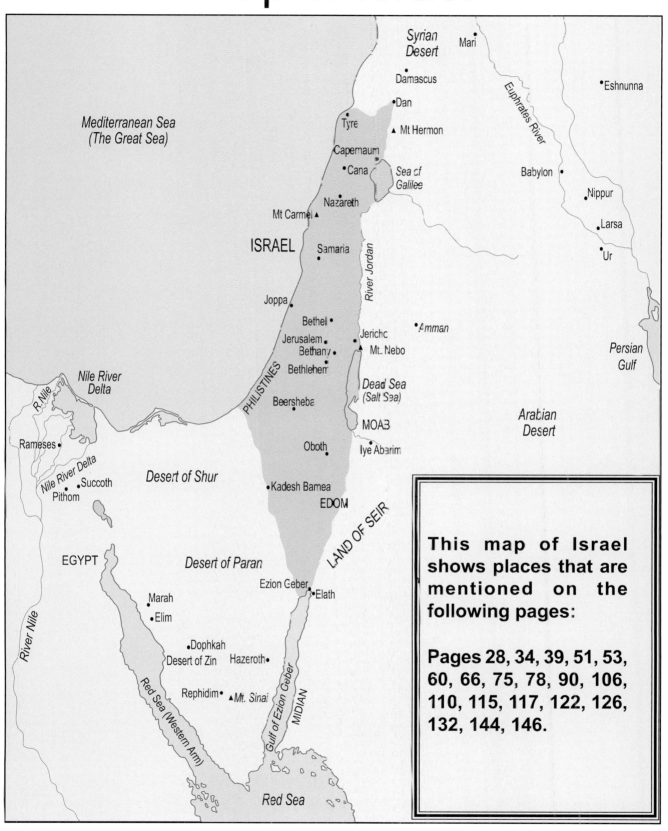

Mediterranean Sea
(The Great Sea)

Syrian Desert

Mari

Damascus

Dan

Tyre

Mt Hermon

Euphrates River

Eshnunna

Capernaum

Cana

Sea of Galilee

Babylon

Nazareth

Nippur

Mt Carmel

Larsa

ISRAEL

Samaria

Ur

River Jordan

Joppa

Bethel

Amman

Jerusalem

Jericho

Bethany

Mt. Nebo

Persian Gulf

Bethlehem

PHILISTINES

Beersheba

Dead Sea
(Salt Sea)

Arabian Desert

MOAB

Oboth

Iye Abarim

Nile River Delta

R. Nile

Rameses

Nile River Delta

Succoth

Pithom

Desert of Shur

Kadesh Barnea

EDOM

LAND OF SEIR

EGYPT

Desert of Paran

Ezion Geber

Elath

Marah

Elim

River Nile

Dophkah

Desert of Zin

Hazeroth

Rephidim

Mt. Sinai

Gulf of Ezion Geber

MIDIAN

Red Sea (Western Arm)

Red Sea

This map of Israel shows places that are mentioned on the following pages:

Pages 28, 34, 39, 51, 53, 60, 66, 75, 78, 90, 106, 110, 115, 117, 122, 126, 132, 144, 146.

Time Line

◁ **Eternity Past**

Creation
(Adam and Eve)

Fall of Man
(Adam and Eve)

Flood of judgement
(Noah)

Fathers of the nation
(Abraham, Isaac and Jacob)

Exile in Egypt - 430 years
(Joseph)

Exodus
(Moses)

Wandering in the wilderness – 40 years
(Moses)

Conquering Canaan – 7 years
(Joshua)

Rule of the Judges – 350 years
(Gideon, Samson, Ruth)

Kingdom of Israel – 110 years
(Samuel, Saul, David, Solomon)

Divided Kingdom – 350 years
(Kings of Judah, Kings of Israel, Jeremiah, Isaiah)

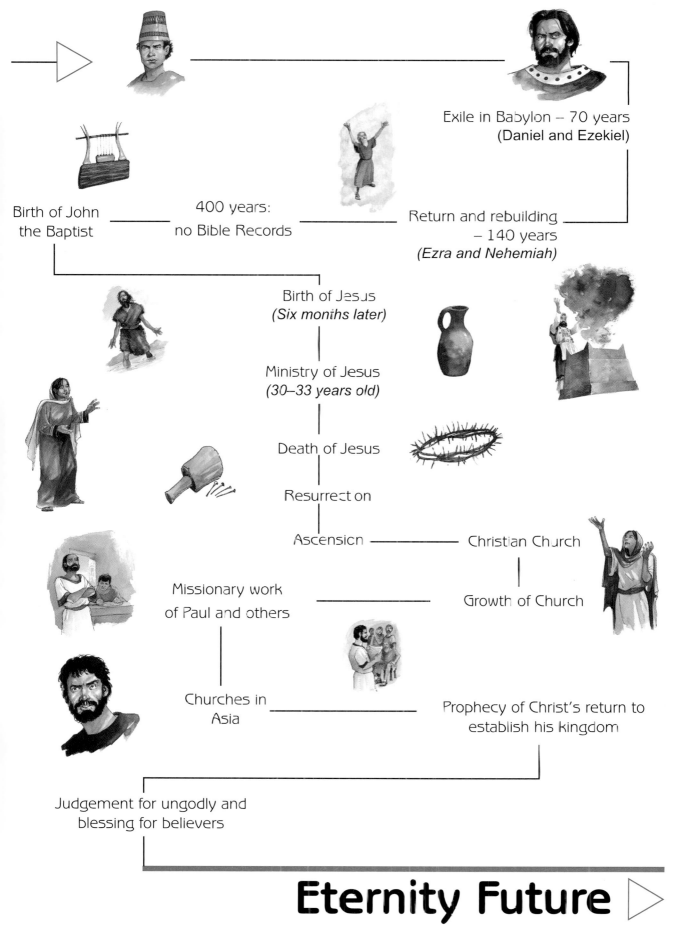

Exile in Babylon – 70 years
(Daniel and Ezekiel)

Birth of John
the Baptist

400 years:
no Bible Records

Return and rebuilding
– 140 years
(Ezra and Nehemiah)

Birth of Jesus
(Six months later)

Ministry of Jesus
(30–33 years old)

Death of Jesus

Resurrection

Ascension —— Christian Church

Growth of Church

Missionary work
of Paul and others

Churches in
Asia

Prophecy of Christ's return to
establish his kingdom

Judgement for ungodly and
blessing for believers

Eternity Future ▷

Contents Page

New Testament Overview

GOSPELS

Matthew

The account of Jesus' life written by Matthew emphasising Jesus as King and Messiah.

Mark

The Gospel written by Mark showing Jesus as servant and miracle worker.

Luke

The Good News from Doctor Luke showing Jesus as the Son of Man.

John

The Gospel written by John with the theme of Jesus as the Son of God.

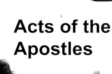

HISTORY

Acts of the Apostles

The history of the early church and how the good news spread to Europe.

EPISTLES

Romans

A letter from Paul to the Christians in Rome.

1 & 2 Corinthians

Two letters to the church in Corinth, from Paul.

Galatians

A letter from Paul to the church in Galatia.

Ephesians

A letter from Paul to Christians in Ephesus.

Philippians

A letter written to the church in Philippi by Paul.

Colossians

A letter written to the church in Colosse by Paul.

1 & 2 Thessalonians

Two letters sent to Christians in Thessalonica by Paul.

EPISTLES cont.

1 & 2 Timothy

Two letters from Paul to Timothy who was a young Christian and friend of Paul.

Titus

A letter from Paul to Titus who was a minister in Crete.

Philemon

A letter written by Paul to Philemon asking for a favour. This letter was written from Rome where Paul was a prisoner.

Hebrews

A letter written to Hebrew believers.

James

A letter from James to Christians in different parts of the world.

1 & 2 Peter

Two letters from Peter to churches in different towns.

1, 2 & 3 John

Three letters from the apostle John to the church generally and Christian friends.

Jude

A letter from Jude to Christian friends.

PROPHECY

Revelation

John's account of visions he had received from God while on the isle of Patmos about the future of the church.

John the Baptist's Birth

Zechariah was a priest at the temple. He and his wife Elizabeth loved the Lord God and lived holy lives. They were getting older and still had no children though they had often prayed for a child. They must have wondered if their prayers would ever be answered.

See next paragraph

One day when Zechariah was working in the temple an angel appeared on the right side of the altar. Zechariah was very afraid. The angel said, "Do not be frightened, Zechariah. Your prayer has been heard. Your wife Elizabeth shall have a baby son and you shall call him John."

Page 107

The angel also told Zechariah that his son would bring joy to many people and through John's preaching people would turn from their sins to love the Lord.

Zechariah could hardly believe his ears. "I am an old man and my wife is old too," he said. The angel replied, "My name is Gabriel and God has sent me to tell you this good news. Because you don't believe me you will be made dumb and not able to speak until my words come true."

Zechariah was not able to speak another word. He came out of the temple and was only able to make signs.

Before long Elizabeth was expecting a baby. She was very pleased. Six months later she had a visit from her cousin Mary. Mary had just received wonderful news from the angel Gabriel that she would be the mother of Jesus, the Son of God.

Next paragraph

As soon as Mary came into Elizabeth's house she called out a greeting to her. Elizabeth felt her baby move inside for joy.

Page 105

Fact File

Luke: The Gospel of Luke was written by Luke who was a doctor.

Babies names: In Bible times it was a custom to name the baby son after his father.

The Priest's job: He had to act as 'go-between' for God and his people. They offered special sacrifices and offerings in the temple to ask God to forgive the people's sin and taught God's laws to the people.

The Holy Spirit: The Holy Spirit is a member of the Trinity. The Trinity consists of three persons – God the Father, God the Son (Jesus Christ) and God the Holy Spirit. These three are one God, the same in substance, equal in power and glory.

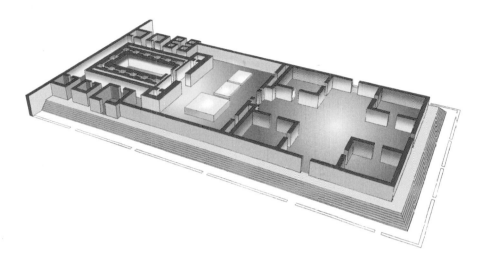

Computer generated reconstruction of Jerusalem Temple

Salvation

 X

Think Spot

:)

Page 108

Elizabeth's baby was a special child. Before he was even born, God the Holy Spirit had made him respond to the Lord Jesus Christ.

Elizabeth was very happy when her baby boy was born. Her neighbours and relations were also glad when they heard how good the Lord had been to her. When the baby was eight days old the time came for him to be named. Some family friends thought that his name should be Zechariah after his father. But Elizabeth said, "Oh no, he shall be called John." The friends objected saying, "None of your relations are called John." They then asked Zechariah what he wanted to call his son. Zechariah signalled for something to write on, and he wrote, "His name is John."

Immediately Zechariah was able to speak again and he praised God. Zechariah told the people that the baby John would be a preacher one day, warning about sin and pointing people to the Messiah. Zechariah knew this about his son because he had been told by God, the Holy Spirit. The Messiah was of course the Lord, Jesus Christ.

P

Fulfillment on page 110

Think Spot

The Holy Spirit made John the Baptist respond to Jesus Christ even before he was born. We all need the Holy Spirit to work in us and to make us love and respond to Jesus Christ whatever our age. Ask the Holy Spirit to do this amazing work in your life.

Salvation

 X

Page 107

Memory Verse

There is rejoicing in the presence of the angels of God over one sinner who repents (Luke 15:10).

Bible Explorer

Birth of Jesus

The Roman Emperor, Caesar Augustus, told everyone in the empire to go back to their home town to be enrolled. Mary and her husband Joseph had to travel from Nazareth to Bethlehem, Joseph's home town. When they arrived the town was so busy, there

P Fulfillment from page 92

was no room for them at the inn. Because of this they sheltered in a stable. Mary's baby boy was born there, in a stable, in Bethlehem. This was the fulfillment of the prophet Micah's prophecy, many years before, that the town of Bethlehem would be the birth place of the Messiah.

Mary then carefully wrapped Jesus in swaddling clothes and laid him in a manger, a feeding box for animals.

Near Bethlehem shepherds watched over their sheep when suddenly an angel appeared and the bright shining light of the glory of the Lord dazzled them. They were afraid.

Page 110

Fact File

Swaddling Clothes: Strips of cloth which were wrapped around new born infants.

Three Wise Men? Mary and Joseph eventually moved out of the stable and into a house. There could have been more than three Wise men visiting them as the Bible doesn't say how many there were. There were however three gifts.

Matthew lists the ancestors of Jesus. Here are some:

Abraham — See Page 20

Rahab — See Page 52

Ruth — See Page 60

David — See Page 68

Bethlehem today

"Don't be afraid," the angel said, "I bring good news for you and all people. Today a Saviour has been born in Bethlehem. He is Christ the Lord. You will find him lying in a manger."

Salvation

Page 109

The shepherds went to Bethlehem and saw the baby for themselves. They passed on the good news to everyone they met. They praised and worshipped God as they went back to work.

Paragraph below

Some time later, wise men from the east came to look for Jesus. They had seen a special star in the sky which had prompted them to look for the King of the Jews in Jerusalem. King Herod was worried. His religious leaders informed him, "The Scriptures tell us that the Messiah will be born in Bethlehem." Herod sent the wise men to Bethlehem with instructions to come back when they had found the baby.

Page 115

The wise men were guided by the star right to the house where Jesus was. They fell down before him and worshipped him. They knew he was God the Son. They gave him beautiful gifts of gold, frankincense and myrrh. Then, God warned the wise men not to go back to Herod. They listened to this warning and went home another way.

Think Spot

The shepherds met the Lord Jesus Christ and were so enthusiastic about him they just had to tell everybody they met. How enthusiastic are you about Jesus? Do you talk about him to your friends?

Memory Verse

Glory to God in the highest, and on earth peace to men on whom his favour rests (Luke 2:14).

Childhood of Jesus

Joseph was warned by the angel of the Lord of danger to the baby Jesus. "Take Jesus and Mary to Egypt. Stay there until I tell you it is safe to return. King Herod wants to destroy the young child." So, in the dead of night, Mary, Joseph and Jesus left Israel for the country of Egypt.

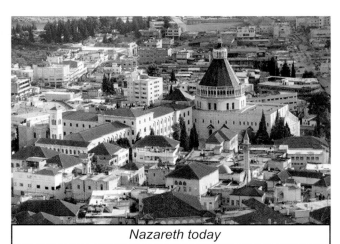
Nazareth today

After Herod died, an angel told Joseph, "Take the child and his mother back to Israel. It is safe now." Joseph took his family back to Nazareth where Jesus grew up. Eventually Mary and Joseph had other children who were brothers and sisters for Jesus. Jesus had four brothers, James, Joseph, Simon and Judas and at least two sisters whose names we are not told. Jesus was a wise and good Page 118 ☺ boy who lived in a way that pleased God, his heavenly Father. He is the only person who has never sinned.

Passover Feast

Every year Jesus' parents went to Jerusalem for the Passover Feast. When he was twelve years old Jesus went too.

After the feast Mary and Joseph set off for home. Jesus stayed behind in Jerusalem on his own. Mary and Joseph assumed that Jesus was with other friends. After they had travelled for a day, they realised he was missing. Back they went to Jerusalem to look for him.

They looked anxiously for three days before they found Jesus in the temple. He was sitting with the teachers listening to them and asking questions. Everyone was amazed at his knowledge.

☹ Page 112

Examples of carpenter's tools

Fact File

Passover: A special Jewish feast commemorating the night when the Israelites painted blood on their door posts. As a result the Angel of Death "passed over" the houses of the Israelites and they were saved. 👁 Page 39

Mary scolded him when she saw him. "Why did you do this? We were so worried."
"Why were you searching for me?" Jesus replied. "Did you not know that I had to be in my Father's house?" They did not understand that he meant God his Father.

Jesus went back to Nazareth with them and was obedient to Mary and Joseph. He grew up to be strong and healthy in mind, body and spirit. God was pleased with him. Jesus helped with the family carpentry business making various things out of wood and using carpentry tools and then began his public ministry at thirty years of age.

 **Think Spot**

Jesus showed obedience to his parents and obedience to God. His ultimate act of obedience was submitting to death on the cross. He knew that this was the only way to save those who believed and trusted in him.

Salvation
Page 110

Memory Verse

And Jesus grew in wisdom and stature, and in favour with God and men (Luke 2:52).

Baptism of Jesus

John the Baptist was Jesus' cousin. He was a preacher who told the people to turn from their sins. He was preparing the way for the Lord Jesus. "I am not the Christ," he said. "I am just a voice crying in the wilderness. The man coming after me *(meaning Jesus)* is much more important than me."

P Fulfilled from page 105

John was called "the Baptist" because many people were baptised by him in the River Jordan. They confessed their sins and were sorry for them. Being baptised in the water was an outward symbol of their sins being washed away.

Salvation **X** Page 112

One day Jesus came to the River Jordan to see John. He asked John to baptise him. John was surprised. "I need to be baptised by you and yet you are coming to me?"

Jesus persuaded him that this was the right thing to do. Jesus had no sin, so his baptism did not mean that his sins had been washed away. His baptism is an example to others and shows us that although he was God, he was also fully man.

Page 128

When Jesus came up out of the water of the River Jordan, the heavens opened up and God the Holy Spirit came down upon him shaped like a dove. The voice of God the Father was heard from heaven saying, "This is my Son, whom I love; with him I am well pleased."

Fact File

Temptation: Temptation itself is not sin. Yielding to temptation is sin. Jesus was tempted. He understands how we feel when we are tempted to sin (Hebrews 4:15).

Trinity: There is only one God. There are three persons in this one God; God the Father; God the Son; God the Holy Spirit. This is called the Trinity.

Temptation of Jesus

After his baptism Jesus was led by the Spirit into the wilderness – a quiet, lonely place. He was there for forty days fasting. He felt very hungry. There the devil met him and tempted him to do wrong. The devil first asked him to prove he was the Son of God by turning stones into bread. Jesus did not give in. He used the Scriptures to fight back.

> **"Man shall not live by bread alone but by every word that comes from the mouth of God," (Deuteronomy 8:3).**

The devil tried again. "Prove you are the Son of God by throwing yourself off the highest part of the temple. Doesn't God say that he will give his angels to help you." Jesus again refused to please the devil. Again he quoted God's word.

> **"Do not put the Lord your God to the test," (Deuteronomy 6:16).**

The devil tried a third time. He took Jesus up a high mountain and showed him the kingdoms of the world. "Fall down and worship me," he said, "and I will give them all to you."

Jesus refused and again he quoted scripture.

> **"Worship the Lord your God and serve Him only," (Deuteronomy 6:13).**

The devil then left Jesus. Angels came to attend to Him.

> **During his temptation Christ used the Scriptures to ward off the devil's attacks. Have another look at the verses he used.**
>
> **"Man shall not live by bread alone but by every word that comes from the mouth of God," (Deuteronomy 8:3).**
> **"Do not put the Lord your God to the test," (Deuteronomy 6:16).**
> **"Worship the Lord your God and serve Him only," (Deuteronomy 6:13).**
>
> **It is good for us to learn Scripture too. The Holy Spirit can remind us of what we have learned. God's word is an excellent tool to use against the devil. It is your best weapon. Use it like Jesus did.**

Think Spot Jesus was tempted just as we are yet he didn't sin. Think about Jesus when you feel tempted. He knows how you feel. Thank Jesus for how he didn't give in to sin. His people will in the end have victory over sin because of him.

Memory Verse

And a voice from heaven said, 'This is my Son, whom I love; with him I am well pleased.' (Matthew 3:17).

Death of John the Baptist

John the Baptist spoke out against sin during the time that King Herod was the ruler in Israel. Herod was a sinful man and John the Baptist knew that he had to tell him this. John the Baptist was a prophet of God. He had to give God's message to the people. God's message to Herod was that his sin was offensive and that he should stop.

Page 42

What had Herod done? He had broken the seventh commandment. Herod's wife's name was Herodias and she was actually the wife of Herod's brother. John told Herod that what he was doing was against God's law. This made Herod very angry indeed. He did not like to be told he was a sinner.

Page 117

John was then thrown in prison where he might have been killed were it not for one thing. King Herod was afraid of the people. Many of the Jews believed that John was a man of God. Herod knew that if he killed John then a riot might start. Herod did not want his subjects to revolt against him. So John remained alive but in prison.

While John was still imprisoned he heard about the wonderful work that Jesus was doing in the country. Jesus even sent his cousin John a message. Jesus told John's friends, 'Tell John about the things you have seen and heard. The blind see, the lame walk, the lepers are cleansed and the deaf hear, the dead are raised to life and the poor have the gospel preached to them.'

When John heard this wonderful news he was certain that Jesus was the Son of God. One day something awful happened. King Herod invited many important guests to his palace for an important party. Herodias' daughter performed a special dance for King Herod and his guests. King Herod was so pleased with her dancing that he said, "I will give you anything you ask for, even half of my kingdom."

The young woman decided to ask her mother for advice. Once she had done this she went to King Herod and demanded to have, "the head of John the Baptist on a big plate."

Fact File

Guilty conscience: Later Herod was bothered with a guilty conscience. He heard about the amazing things that Jesus was doing and he was afraid it was John the Baptist raised from the dead.

Gospel: This is another name given to the Good News of Jesus Christ. The Good News is that Jesus Christ has come to save us from our sins.

Salvation

☒

Think Spot

Herod, who did not want to look stupid in front of his friends, granted her request. John the Baptist was beheaded. His head was placed on a large plate and the young girl took it and presented it to her mother. John the Baptist's friends took his body from the prison and buried it. Then they went to tell Jesus all that had happened.

Think Spot

All his life John the Baptist loved the Lord Jesus Christ. His great work was to warn people about their sin and to tell them of Jesus Christ their Saviour. Will you follow John the Baptist's advice and look to Jesus?

Salvation

Memory Verse

Memory Verse

Look, the Lamb of God, who takes away the sin of the world (John 1:29).

Salvation

Page 114

Calling of Disciples

Salvation

[X]

Page
115

Jesus started to preach the good news or gospel of God in Galilee. "The Kingdom of God is near. Repent and believe the good news."

As Jesus walked beside the Sea of Galilee he noticed two fishermen, Simon and his brother Andrew throwing a fishing net into the lake. "Come follow me," Jesus said, "and I will make you fishers of men."

At once they left their nets and followed Jesus. They were his first disciples. Jesus gave Simon a new name - Peter, which means a rock. A little further on he met two other fishermen, James and his brother John. Jesus called to them to follow him. They both left their father Zebedee in the boat with the hired men and followed Jesus.

Levi was a tax collector. One day he was sitting in his collector's booth. Jesus came up to Levi and told him, "Follow me." Levi obeyed immediately. He became one of the disciples. His name was changed to Matthew.

In all Jesus appointed twelve men to be his special followers called disciples. They listened to Jesus and preached the good news of God too.

The Twelve Disciples

***Simon Peter   *Andrew - Simon Peter's brother
*John - Son of Zebedee   *James - John's brother
*Philip   *Bartholomew   *Thomas
*Matthew   *James - Son of Alphaeus
*Thaddaeus or Judas   *Simon the Zealot   *Judas Iscariot**

Jesus' First Miracle

Jesus and his mother Mary were invited to a wedding in Cana in Galilee. Many guests were at the wedding feast including Jesus' disciples.

In the middle of the meal, Mary came to Jesus and said, "The wine is finished. There is no more left." Jesus answered, "Woman, what can I do about that? My time has not come yet." Mary said to the servants, "Do whatever Jesus tells you."

In the room were six big stone water pots used for washing. Jesus told the servants, "Fill the water pots with water." They filled them up to the brim. Then Jesus ordered, "Draw out a cupful and take it to the man in charge of the feast."

When the man drank some, he thought it was the best wine he had ever tasted. He called the bridegroom and congratulated him on the good wine. The servants, who had filled the water pots with water and then drew out the wine, knew that a miracle had been performed that day. This was the first miracle that Jesus did. This showed his power and glory to many people. The disciples believed on him.

 Mary knew who to turn to in a problem. She knew that Jesus would help. Who do you turn to when you need help? Do you pray to God? Do you believe that he can help you? It must have been amazing to see Jesus perform this miracle of changing the water into wine. He does even more amazing miracles. He changes people.

Page 118

Salvation

Page 116

 Memory Verse

"Come, follow me," Jesus said, "and I will make you fishers of men," (Mark 1:17).

Sea of Galilee

Fact File

Water pots: These were there to be used for ceremonial washing. Each was able to hold about 90-120 litres.

Kingdom of God: This means God ruling over the hearts of his people.

People helped by Jesus

One night a Pharisee called Nicodemus came to Jesus. He knew that Jesus was a teacher who had come from God because of the miracles he had done. Jesus said to him, "No-one can see the Kingdom of God unless he is born again." Nicodemus could not understand that.

Nicodemus asked, "How can you be born when you are already old? Your mother can't give birth to you a second time!" Jesus explained, "This is not a natural birth but a spiritual birth." It is not possible to see spiritual birth but it is possible to see the effect of it in a person's life. We cannot see the wind but we can see the effects of the wind and hear the sound of it. It is difficult to understand. Even a clever man like Nicodemus was puzzled. Jesus went on to give the good news of the gospel, "God so loved the world that he gave his one and only Son (*i.e. Jesus Christ*) that whoever believes in him shall not perish but have eternal life."

Salvation

Page 117

Fact File

Pharisee: A member of a religious group who kept the letter of the law very strictly.

Well: An important part of daily life. All water was collected there.

Witness: Telling others about Christ by words or actions.

A Samaritan Woman

Page 122

Jesus was travelling to Galilee through Samaria. Tired, he sat down by a well. A Samaritan woman came to draw water and Jesus asked her for a drink. She was surprised that he spoke to her. Jews didn't usually speak to Samaritans.

Jesus said, "If you knew who asked you for a drink, you would have asked him and he would have given you living water." The woman wondered what he would draw the water with and asked, "Where can you get this living water?" Jesus answered, "Everyone who drinks from this

Salvation

Next Column

well will be thirsty again. But whoever drinks the water I give will never thirst. It will be a spring of water which leads to eternal life." When she asked for this water Jesus told her, "Call your husband and come back."

"I have no husband," she said. Jesus knew that this was true. She had had husbands in the past but was now with a man who wasn't her husband. The woman realised that Jesus was a prophet. She discussed religious differences between the Jews and Samaritans but Jesus directed her mind to the true worship of God. He showed her that he was the promised Messiah,

the Son of God. She believed in him, left her water pot at the well and ran to tell everyone, "Come see a man who knows all about me. Is not this the Christ?" Many people believed on Jesus because of the witness of this woman.

Salvation

Think Spot

The Official's Son

Jesus was visiting Cana in Galilee. A royal official whose son was very sick in Capernaum begged for help. Jesus challenged him, "Unless you people see miraculous signs and wonders you will not believe." The royal official said to him, "Sir, come down before my child dies." Jesus replied, "You may go. Your son will live."

The man believed Jesus and set off for home. When he was met by his servants, they told him his son was alive. He had recovered at the seventh hour of the previous day. The father realised that this was the exact time Jesus had said, "Your son will live." So he and his household believed.

> Think Spot
>
> Jesus knew all about the life of the Samaritan woman. He knows every detail of your life. Jesus was willing to help the Samaritan woman. In what way did he do this? He told her about himself. He told her that through him she could have eternal life.
>
> Salvation
>
> Page 119

Memory Verse — For God so loved the world that he gave his one and only Son, that whoever believes in him shall not perish but have eternal life (John 3:16).

Sermon on the Mount

Fulfilled from page 88

Jesus preached a powerful sermon sitting on a mountain with his disciples around him. This is known as the Sermon on the Mount. He tells what it means to be truly blessed or really happy. Some of the statements he makes are quite surprising.

BEATITUDES

Blessed are the poor in spirit, for theirs is the kingdom of heaven.
Blessed are those who mourn, for they will be comforted.
Blessed are the meek, for they will inherit the earth.
Blessed are those who hunger and thirst for righteousness, for they will be filled.
Blessed are the merciful, for they will be shown mercy.
Blessed are the pure in heart, for they will see God.
Blessed are the peacemakers, for they will be called sons of God.
Blessed are those who are persecuted because of righteousness,
for theirs is the kingdom of heaven
(Matthew 5:3-10).

Jesus gives good practical advice about life. Obeying the letter of the law is not enough. Our attitude to others – the way we feel in our heart – is just as important. Love is vitally important too. It is not enough just to love those who are good to us. Jesus tells us to love even those who are our enemies.

Page 121

Next Column Jesus teaches about prayer. He tells us that we should not show off when we pray, trying to impress other people but that we should talk to God in a quiet secret place. God will answer in the best way. Do not just babble words you have memorised. Really think about what you are praying. God knows what you need. He is keen to listen to you.

Jesus warns us not to be critical of others. We too have faults. When we criticise someone we often have a bigger fault than

Page 121

Jesus taught the special prayer called the Lord's Prayer as an example for us:

*Our Father in heaven
hallowed be your name.
Your kingdom come
your will be done
on earth as it is in heaven.
Give us today our daily bread.
Forgive us our sins as we also
have forgiven those who sin against us.
And lead us not into temptation,
but deliver us from the evil one.
For yours is the kingdom
and the power and the glory
for ever. Amen.*

the person we criticise. Jesus pointed this out when he said: "You tell your friend he has a speck of dust in his eye, when you yourself have a big piece of wood in your eye. Get rid of your own piece of wood before you try to sort out your friend's speck of dust."

The Wise and Foolish Builders

Two men were building houses. One built his house on a rock - a good firm foundation. When the storm came the house was safe and solid. Jesus said that if we hear what God tells us in the Bible and put it into practice in our lives, we are like the wise man in that story. Our lives will be founded on the solid foundation and will stand up to the storms and difficulties of life.

The other man was foolish. He built on sand. When the storm came the foundation was washed away and the house collapsed. If we hear God's word and do not do what he tells us then we are like that foolish man. Our lives will be in ruins too.

Jesus was a wonderful teacher and preacher. People listened to him and were amazed at how he taught with such authority not like the other teachers. Simon Peter admitted that Jesus' words give eternal life.

 Memory Verse

Let everyone who is godly pray (Psalm 32:6).

 Think Spot

The Lord's Prayer reminds us that it is important to forgive others, the same way as he has forgiven us.

Salvation ☒
Page 120

Parables of the Kingdom

To help his followers understand more about his kingdom, Jesus used parables. They were simple stories about everyday activites which made his teaching easier to remember.

One day Jesus went to the Sea of Galilee. A large crowd gathered to listen to him. He got into a boat on the lake to speak while the crowds gathered on the shore.

He told a story about a farmer sowing seed. As he scattered the seed some fell on the path. Birds ate it up. Some fell on rocky ground. They grew quickly because the soil was shallow but when the hot sun shone they shrivelled up because their roots couldn't reach moisture. Other seed fell among thorns which choked it. But some landed on good ground and eventually the farmer got a crop. The people listening were interested in this story. Farming was very important to them. Jesus went on to explain what the story meant.

The seed is like the Word of God. Some hear God's word but the devil makes them forget it quickly. This is like the seed that fell on the path and was eaten by birds. Others hear God's word gladly but when trouble comes they lose interest, like the seed on rocky ground. The seed that fell in the thorns is like people who hear the word but their interest is choked by riches and pleasure. But those who receive God's word, understand it and live by it are like the seed which fell on good ground.

The Weeds

Jesus then told another parable about a farmer's field. One night when everyone slept, an enemy sowed weeds among the good seeds. The field looked good until the plants began to

Thistles amongst corn

grow. The weeds grew alongside the wheat. The farm workers asked if they should pull the weeds out but the farmer explained that this would damage the wheat. It would be better to leave the weeds and wheat growing together until harvest time, then pull out the weeds and burn them and gather the wheat safely into the barn. Jesus explained this story. Jesus sows seed. The field is the world. The good seeds are the people who belong to the kingdom of Jesus. The enemy is the devil. The harvest happens at the Day of Judgement. The angels are the reapers. Those who belong to the devil will be destroyed and those who love the Lord will be safe in heaven.

Salvation

Page123

Memory Verse	The word of God is living and active. Sharper than any double-edged sword ... it judges the thoughts and attitudes of the heart (Hebrews 4:12).

Jesus also told short parables to explain things about his kingdom.

Hidden Treasure

Page 123

A man found treasure in a field. He rushed off, sold all that he had to buy the field. He was so happy that the treasure now belonged to him. It is worth giving up everything else in order to belong to God's kingdom.

Beautiful Pearl

One man saw an extremely beautiful pearl for sale and sold everything in order to buy it. He wanted it so much he thought it was worth it. Belonging to the kingdom is more important than anything else.

> **Think Spot** When you hear the word of God how do you react? Do you refuse to believe it? Do you love the Lord Jesus Christ and follow him? If you follow Jesus Christ, God will help you. Prayer and God's word are valuable sources of help for Christians.
>
> Page 122

Fishing Net

When a fisherman pulls in his nets he catches good and bad fish, he keeps the good but throws the bad back into the sea. By this story Jesus reminds us that at the end of time he will separate those who are in his kingdom and those who are not.

Fact File

Parables: These are simple stories about everyday activites. Jesus used these when teaching the people as they made his lessons easier to remember.

Bible Explorer

Feeding the 5,000

Paragraph Below

Jesus was sad when he heard that John the Baptist had been killed. He and his disciples wanted to get away from the crowds for some rest. So they sailed across the lake to a quiet place. But the crowds followed them by foot. When Jesus got to the quiet place he saw a large crowd wanting to listen to him. He took pity on the people and healed the sick. In the evening the disciples asked Jesus to send the people away to get food. Jesus said, "Can you not give them something to eat?" There was a boy in the crowd who had five small loaves and two fishes. That was all the food they could find. The disciples wondered how such a small amount of food could feed over 5,000 people. Jesus told his disciples to make all the people sit down on the grass. He then

Next Column

took the loaves and fishes and gave thanks to God for them. Jesus broke the loaves and fishes into pieces and handed them to the disciples who gave the food out to all the people. Jesus who is creator of all things had multiplied the food to feed over 5000 people. Afterwards the disciples cleared up and collected twelve baskets full of left over food. Jesus had provided more than enough.

Walking on Water

Then Jesus sent the crowds and disciples away. The disciples rowed across the lake of Galilee. Jesus went to a mountain alone to pray. The disciples had travelled some distance when a storm started. Between 3 am and 6 am Jesus walked towards them on the water. The disciples were terrified and thought it was a ghost. But

Page126

Jesus said, "It is I. Don't be afraid."

Peter replied, "If it is you Lord, tell me to come to you on the water." Jesus told him, "Come." Peter got out of the boat and walked on the water to Jesus. But then he got scared. He cried, "Lord, save me." Immediately Jesus reached out and caught him and said, "You of little faith, why did you doubt?"

Think Spot

The Sea of Galilee

When they got into the boat the wind calmed. The disciples worshipped Jesus saying, "Truly you are the Son of God."

Jesus is still the same. When we are scared we can trust in him – the Son of God.

Jesus Heals

Jairus, a ruler in the Jewish church, came to Jesus and pleaded with him to come and heal his daughter who was dying. Jesus went with Jairus towards his house but there was a delay when Jesus stopped and asked, "Who

Fact File

The Lake of Galilee: Sometimes referred to as The Sea of Galilee. Set between two ranges of high hills it is subject to sudden fierce winds and violent storms.

But then Jairus' servant came with bad news. "Your daughter is dead, do not trouble the Master."

Jesus said, "Do not be afraid, just believe and she will be made better." He took three disciples, Peter, James and John, and the girl's parents with him to her room. He took the girl's hand and said, "Little girl, get up." Immediately she came back to life and got up out of bed. Her parents were overjoyed. Jesus told them to fetch her something to eat. Through faith in Jesus Christ both the little girl and the woman who had been bleeding were restored to health.

Page 128

Salvation

Page 125

touched me?" The disciples wondered why he asked that as there were so many people around. But Jesus knew that power had gone out from him. A frightened woman fell at Jesus' feet and told him her story. "I have been ill for twelve years with internal bleeding. I spent all my money on doctors, but none could help me. But I knew if I touched the hem of your garment, I would be healed. As soon as I touched it I was healed." Jesus comforted her saying, "Daughter, your faith has healed you, go in peace."

Salvation

Next Column

Memory Verse

Jesus Christ is the same yesterday, today and for ever (Hebrews 13:8).

Think Spot

Thank God for your food. Many today know what it is like to have no food. Jesus also knew what this felt like. Don't forget to thank God for the food you eat today.

Page 124

Jesus The Teacher

Transfiguration

Page 126

One day Jesus took Peter, James and John up a mountain to pray. While they watched him, Jesus changed. His face shone as bright as the sun. His clothes became as white as light. They saw Moses and Elijah talking with him. Then a bright cloud covered them and they heard a voice saying about Jesus, "This is my Son, whom I love, with him I am well pleased. Listen to him." This was God's voice. Peter, James and John were so afraid, they fell to the ground. Jesus came and touched them. When they looked up they saw that Jesus was alone. "Do not tell anyone about this," Jesus said "until the Son of man (Jesus Christ) is risen from the dead." Peter, James and John wondered what he meant by "rising from the dead."

Teaching

The disciples asked Jesus, "Who is the greatest in the kingdom of heaven?" To help them understand his answer Jesus called a child over to stand beside him. "Unless you become like this little child you will never enter the kingdom of heaven," he said. "The greatest in the kingdom is the one who is as humble as this little child. The person who welcomes a little child like this one, is really welcoming me."

Children were brought by their parents to Jesus so that he would put his hands on them and pray. The disciples were annoyed and tried to send them away. "Let the children come to me," Jesus demanded. "Don't stop them. The kingdom of heaven belongs to them and other children like them." Jesus placed his hands on them and blessed them.

Some people tried to trick Jesus by putting unhelpful questions to him about the law of God. Jesus always answered wisely.

"Which is the first commandment of all?" he was asked one day. Jesus' reply was "You shall love the Lord your God with all your heart and with all your soul and with all your mind and with all your strength: this is the first commandment. The second one is "You shall love your neighbour as yourself." This summarises the ten commandments that God gave to his people from Mount Sinai through Moses.

Page 42

A man asked Jesus, "How often should I forgive my brother, if he sins – as many as seven times?" "No," said Jesus. "Seventy times seven times." Forgiveness is very important. We must show forgiveness to others if we wish to be forgiven.

Memory Verse

If ... you seek the Lord your God, you will find him if you look for him with all your heart (Deuteronomy 4:29).

Fact File

Transfiguration: Means to change appearance.

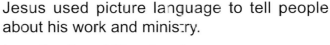

Jesus used picture language to tell people about his work and ministry.

I am the **Good Shepherd.**
This shows Christ's love and care for those who follow him.

I am the **Bread of Life**.
Jesus used these words to show the feeding and nourishment that he gives to the soul. Jesus also reminded them of the manna that God had given to his people  long ago.

Page 40

I am the **Door.**
This shows us that it is only through him we can gain access to God the Father.

I am the **Light of the World.**
This shows us that Jesus Christ will lead us and give us guidance and safety.

I am the **True Vine** and you are the branches.
These words show us how we depend on Jesus Christ for life.

I am the **Way the Truth and the Life.**
No one comes to God the Father except through me. Jesus Christ used these words to show that he is the only way to God.

Salvation

Think
Spot

Think Spot

Some people do not believe that Jesus is the only way to God. But it is true. Jesus Christ says so himself. He is the way, the truth and the life. He is the only way to God and eternal life. God says that those who look for him will find him.

Salvation

Page 126

People Jesus Met

The Family at Bethany

Martha and Mary and their brother Lazarus were a family who lived in Bethany. They were friends of Jesus. Sometimes he came to their house for a meal. One time Martha was busy preparing a meal for Jesus. Her sister Mary was sitting at Jesus' feet listening to his wise teaching. Martha was upset that she had all the work to do. "Ask my sister to help me," she complained.

Page129

"Martha, Martha," Jesus replied, "you are worried and anxious about lots of things. But Mary has decided to do the best thing."

Some time later Mary and Martha were very worried because Lazarus was ill. "Let's send for Jesus," they suggested. "He will help."

Jesus Comes to Bethany

Jesus received their message but did not immediately rush to Bethany. Lazarus had died by the time he arrived. He had been buried for four days. As soon as Martha heard that Jesus was near she rushed to meet him. Mary stayed at home. "If only you had been here, Lazarus would not have died," she exclaimed to Jesus.

"Your brother will rise again," Jesus assured her. Martha returned to the house to tell Mary that Jesus had come. Mary greeted Jesus with the same sad message. They took Jesus to the place where Lazarus was buried. Jesus wept there. To everyone's amazement Jesus ordered, "Take the stone away." The stone was moved. Jesus prayed to God the Father, then shouted loudly, "Lazarus, come out." Lazarus walked out of the grave still wearing the linen grave clothes. Mary and Martha were overjoyed. Many people who saw this miracle for themselves, believed in Jesus and became his followers.

Paragraph Below

Salvation

Page 127

A tomb with a stone rolled away from the entrance.

Blind Bartimaeus

Bartimaeus was blind. He could not work. He just sat by the roadside in Jericho begging. News was passed through the crowd that Jesus was coming along the road. Bartimaeus started to shout, "Jesus, Son of David, have mercy on me!" Some people told him to be quiet. But he shouted even more loudly "Have mercy on me."

Page 131

Think Spot

To become a follower of Jesus you do not have to become a better person first. Zacchaeus was a scoundrel. When he trusted in Jesus Christ, his new life began.

Jesus stopped and said, "Call him over." So they called Bartimaeus. "Cheer up. Get up. Jesus is calling for you."

Bartimaeus threw aside his cloak, jumped up and came to Jesus.

"What do you want me to do for you?" Jesus asked. "I want to see again," he replied.

"Your faith has healed you," Jesus told him. He could see at once, and followed Jesus down the road.

Zacchaeus

Crowds of people lined the streets of Jericho to see Jesus. Zacchaeus, a chief tax collector, wanted to see Jesus too but was not tall enough to look over the heads of the people. He was so keen that he ran along the road and climbed a sycamore tree to get a good view. Jesus looked up at him and said, "Hurry down Zacchaeus. I want to come to your house today."

Zacchaeus was delighted to welcome Jesus to his home. The people grumbled. Zacchaeus was not popular. He was a rich man but had gained his wealth by cheating and charging too much tax money. When Zacchaeus met Jesus he changed.

"I will give half of my wealth to the poor," he told Jesus. "If I cheated anyone I will give back four times as much."

Salvation
Page 128

Jesus said, "Salvation has come to this house today. The Son of Man came to seek and to save the lost."

Memory Verse

Jesus wept (John 11:35).

Fact File

Shortest verse in the Bible: The memory verse on this page is actually the shortest verse in the Bible, John 11:35.

Mercy: Gracious love and pity shown by God to undeserving sinners.

Bible Explorer

Parables

Jesus explained to the Pharisees that sinners were important to him. He told them stories or parables to show how God finds lost sinners.

The Lost Sheep

Page 130

Paragraph below

Salvation

Paragraph below

A man had one hundred sheep, but lost one. The man left the ninety-nine sheep to search for it. He didn't give up. When the lost sheep was found he was overjoyed. He told his friends and they all celebrated. In the same way there is joy in heaven every time Jesus finds a sinner.

The Lost Coin

Another parable was about a woman who had ten precious coins. One day she lost one. She searched carefully with a lamp and swept with a brush in every corner of her house till she found it. When she found it she was delighted. She told her neighbours who rejoiced with her. Jesus tells us that the angels in heaven are very happy when one lost sinner is found by him.

Page 133

Salvation

Page 129

Think Spot

A person who does not believe in Jesus Christ is a lost sinner. Jesus tells us that when God judges the world at the last day, lost sinners will be sent to a terrible place called Hell.

The Lost Son

Jesus told another story about the joy in heaven when someone is converted. It is about a father who had two sons. The oldest son worked on his father's farm; the younger son wanted to leave home and see the world. So he asked his father if he could have his share of his father's money. His father agreed. The younger son left home. He travelled around, enjoying parties and spending all his money. He was popular with people because he had money. One day there was no money left. He had spent it all.

A famine came to the land. The young son was now without money or food, he had to get work looking after pigs. He felt so hungry that he could have eaten the pig's food. Then he started to think.

"Here I am starving to death while my father's servants have plenty to eat. I will go back to my father and admit that I have sinned against him and against God. I will ask him if I can become one of his servants because I am not worthy to be his son."

So he started off for home. His father saw him coming from a distance. He ran towards him and welcomed him with open arms.

The young son confessed that he had done wrong, saying how he was no longer worthy to be called his son.

Fact File

Pharisees: A religious group of Jews, who were very formal and bigoted. Jesus often denounced them for their hypocrisy.

But his father ordered his servants to bring out special clothes and prepare a special meal. He wanted to celebrate saying, "My son was dead, but now is alive. He was lost and is found."

The older son had been out working all day, he came home to find the noise of a party. He asked what was going on. He was told by one of the servants the good news, that they were celebrating the return of his younger brother.

This made him so angry that he would not go into the house and join in the celebrations. His father came out and reasoned with him.
 Page132

The older son told him how he felt. He was jealous that the younger son who had wasted so much money was being treated so specially while he who had worked faithfully never got a party arranged for him.

His father gently replied, "My son, you are always with me, and all that I have is yours. It is right for us to celebrate and be glad because your brother was as **Salvation** Page 131
good as dead and is now alive, he was lost but is now found."

Jesus told this story because he wanted the Pharisees to know about the love that God has for sinners, that those who repent and return to God are welcomed with open arms.

Memory Verse

The Son of Man came to seek and to save what was lost (Luke 19:10).

More Parables

The Good Samaritan

A lawyer asked Jesus what he had to do to gain eternal life. Jesus said, "What do you read in God's Word about that?" The man answered, "God's Word tells us to love God with all our heart, soul, strength and mind and also love our neighbour as ourselves." Jesus told him he was correct. But the lawyer asked, "Who is my neighbour?" Jesus explained by using a parable.

A man travelled on a dangerous road from Jerusalem to Jericho. He was attacked by thieves who left him beaten up by the roadside. A priest came along, saw the man and hurried on as fast as he could. A Levite came next, also a religious man. He did not help either. But walked quickly away. The next person to see the poor man was a Samaritan. Jews and Samaritans did not normally speak to each other, but this one took pity on the hurting man, gave him first aid, put him on to his donkey and took him to a nearby inn. He even stayed a night to look after him. Next day the Samaritan gave money to the inn keeper to look after the man till he was well enough to carry on. Any extra costs he would repay next time he was passing.

Page 131

Jesus then asked the lawyer, "Which person was a neighbour to the hurt man?" The lawyer knew it was the Samaritan who had been kind. So Jesus told him, "You should do the same."

Think Spot Prayer that pleases God must come from our heart. The words that the Pharisee said were not true prayer. He was proud of himself and wanted to tell God how good he was. It is much more honest to pray like the tax-collector, asking God for forgiveness.

Memory Verse

God have mercy on me, a sinner (Luke 18:13).

The Good Shepherd

Page 132

Jesus uses a story of a shepherd and his sheep to explain something of the relationship between himself and his people.

Jesus is the good shepherd, the sheep know his voice and will follow him. Sheep will run away from strangers because

Salvation

Page 132

they are afraid, but they trust their shepherd. The shepherd makes sure his sheep are safe. Jesus gave his life for his people.

A hired worker would get scared and run off when great danger from wild animals came, but because the sheep belong to the shepherd he is prepared to give his life for the sheep. The good shepherd knows his sheep and his sheep know him. Jesus knows his people and loves them so much that he gave his life for them. Jesus died to save sinners.

The Tax Collector's Prayer

Jesus told this parable to those who were proud of their good deeds and looked down on others. The parable is about two men who went to the temple to pray, one was a Pharisee the other a tax collector. The Pharisee was proud of himself and thought he was very good. When he prayed he prayed about himself.

Fact File

"God I thank you that I am not greedy, dishonest or immoral like other people. I am not like that tax collector. I fast twice a week and give a tenth of my money to you." He was being very smug.

Page 136

The tax collector was different, he knew he was a sinner. He bowed his head and prayed, "God have mercy on me a sinner."

Jesus then explained that the tax collector's prayer was real and from his heart. He was forgiven by God, but the Pharisee was not. We must see that we are sinners and ask God to show mercy on us.

Fact File

Fasting: To go without food at a time of crisis or repentance. Jesus pointed out that some people fasted for show and were hypocritical. God wants heart felt love and obedience to him rather than false shows of loyalty.

Samaritan: A person from Samaria - a country between Judea and Galilee. The people from Samaria had a long-standing feud with the Jewish people.

To Jerusalem

Jesus asked his disciples one day, "Whom do people say I am?"

"Some think you are John the Baptist, Elijah or a great prophet come back to life," they replied.

"And whom do you say I am?" he asked. Peter spoke. "You are the Christ, the Son of the Living God." God had revealed this truth to Peter. From then on Jesus warned his disciples that he would go to Jerusalem. There he would suffer greatly, then be killed. That was not defeat. This was the great work of salvation for his people. He would rise again on the third day.

Salvation

Page 135

Jesus and the disciples then headed for Jerusalem. When they came near the Mount of Olives, Jesus called two of his disciples over. "Go to that village over there," he said. "You will find a young donkey tethered. It has never been ridden. Untie him and bring him to me. If anyone asks you what you are doing tell them that the Lord needs this donkey."

Page 135

The two disciples found the animal just as Jesus had described, tied outside the house. The owners did indeed ask what they were doing. The answer, "The Lord needs him" satisfied them fully.

The disciples brought the young donkey and put some of their clothes on its back. Jesus rode into Jerusalem. Crowds joined the procession. Some cut down palm branches and placed them on the road in front of Jesus. Others laid down their cloaks. The crowd shouted out joyfully, "Hosanna to the Son of David. Blessed is the king that comes in the name of the Lord." Jesus rode into town, hearing the shouts of triumph and praise.

Fulfilled from
Page 93

Not everyone was pleased. Some of the church leaders complained. Jesus was pleased. "It is right that they shout out praise," he said.

Page 136

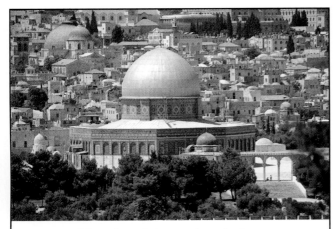

The city of Jerusalem today.

Think Spot

Children were in the crowd who shouted praise to Jesus in Jerusalem. They realised that Jesus was truly God and ought to be worshipped. You are not too young to worship Jesus.

Memory Verse

O Lord, save us; O Lord, grant us success (Psalm 118:25).

The next day in the temple Jesus chased away the greedy men who were using the temple as a trading place. He overturned the tables of the money changers and the benches of those selling doves. The little children sang praise and cheered Jesus. Jesus was delighted to hear them. He made blind people see again and lame people walk.

Page 140

Fact File

Christ: This is the Greek word for "anointed one". It has the same meaning as the Hebrew word "Messiah".

Hosanna: Hebrew word meaning "Please save." Quoting Psalm 118:25. An appropriate shout of prayer to Jesus on his way to the crucifixion.

Bible Explorer

Judas' Plot

A wicked plot was hatched to kill Jesus. Many religious leaders hated him. Judas Iscariot, one of Jesus' disciples, offered to help them catch Jesus. They agreed to give him thirty pieces of silver if he would betray Jesus. From then on he looked out for the opportunity to turn Jesus over to his enemies.

Passover Feast

It was time for the Passover Feast, Jesus sent two of his disciples to get it ready. "Follow the man you meet who will be carrying a jar of water," said Jesus. "He will lead you to a house. Explain to the owner that we will need a room to eat the Passover Feast. He will show you to a large upstairs room. Get everything ready there."

They followed his instructions, and in the evening Jesus arrived with the rest of the disciples.

Fact File

Fetching Water: This was usually a woman's work. It was unusual for a man to be seen carrying a water jar from the well. This meant he was easy for the disciples to spot in the crowd.

Passover: The feast reminding God's people of his goodness to them in Egypt. The angel of death "passed over" the house which had the blood of the lamb on the door post. This happened just before they were allowed to leave Egypt. God told them to keep the Passover feast every year from that time on.

Page 39

The Last Supper

Page 39

The Passover Feast took on a new meaning that night. Jesus was preparing himself and his followers for his death.

He broke the bread and handed it round. "This is my body," he said. Then he passed round a cup of wine. "This is my blood," he said. "When you eat the bread and drink the wine, remember me."

We call this the Lord's Supper or Communion. Followers of Jesus all over the world still remember him in this way. The broken bread and the poured out wine are meant to make us think

Salvation
X
Page 137

of Jesus' body and blood, and how he suffered for his people on the cross.

Jesus knew that Judas was thinking of betraying him. During the meal he said, "One of you shall betray me."

The disciples naturally wanted to know who would do such a dreadful thing. "Lord, tell us who it is," one of them said.

"It is the man to whom I shall give this piece of food," he replied, handing a piece of bread to Judas Iscariot.

Judas immediately slunk out of the room into the dead of night.

Jesus spoke for many hours with his friends, warning them of the difficult days ahead. "I will never let you down," Peter stated boldly.

Jesus sadly replied, "Before the cock crows twice tomorrow morning, you will have denied three times that you know me."

Page 136

They sang a psalm of praise before going out into the night.

Think Spot

Have you ever been at a Communion Service when those who love the Lord Jesus Christ eat some bread and drink some wine, the symbols of Jesus' body and blood? When they do this, they are obeying the instructions of the Lord Jesus to all his followers.

Memory Verse

This is my body given for you; do this in remembrance of me (Luke 22:19).

Bible Explorer

Gethsemane

Page 138

Jesus and the disciples went to a garden called Gethsemane. "Sit here," he said, "while I go over there to pray." He took Peter, James and John with him. "I am troubled," he said. "Stay here and keep me company."

Garden of Gethsemane today.

He went a little further on and fell down on his face, praying to God his Father.

When he came back to his disciples, he found them sleeping. "Why are you sleeping?" he asked. "Get up and pray."

Just then, Judas Iscariot came up with a crowd of men. He greeted Jesus with a kiss - not a sign of love or friendship but a pre-arranged signal to the enemies of Jesus who wanted to have Jesus arrested.

The disciples went to fight. One of them lashed out with a sword and cut off the ear of the high priest's servant.

Jesus said, "No more of this!" He touched the man's ear and it was healed immediately.

The crowd of men arrested Jesus and led him away to the high priest's house.

High Priest's Home

Jesus endured a mockery of a trial at Caiaphas' house. The witnesses statements did not agree. They accused him of blasphemy, because he told them the truth, that he was the Son of God. They spat on his face. They mocked and jeered.

Meanwhile Peter was in the courtyard, warming himself by the fire. A servant girl recognised him. "This man was with Jesus," she said.

"I don't know him," snapped Peter angrily. He moved out to the porch just as the cock crowed once.

Later someone else said "Are you one of them?"

"I am not," said Peter hotly. "I do not know this man."

Page 140

An hour later someone else said, "I am sure this man was with Jesus - he is a Galilean too."

"I do not know what you are talking about," replied Peter in a panic.

Just at that moment the cockerel crew for the second time at day break. Jesus looked over to Peter and caught his eye. How ashamed Peter felt. He went out and wept bitterly. He had let Jesus down. He had denied him.

Page 155

Fact File

The Garden of Gethsemane: This was situated near Jerusalem. Jesus and his disciples often met there. This garden of olive trees is still there today.

 Jesus was sent to Pilate, the Roman Governor. He could find no fault with him. King Herod questioned him and cruelly mocked him then sent him back to Pilate. Pilate wanted to release Jesus. He usually released a prisoner during the feast week.
However, Pilate weakly gave in to public opinion.
Barabbas the robber was released. Jesus was sent
to be crucified.

 Think Spot How ashamed Peter felt after he had denied the Lord Jesus. He wept tears of repentance. The Lord Jesus forgave him. God is the same today. He still forgives sinners who repent. Peter went on to become a brave preacher of the Gospel.

Salvation

X

Page138

Memory Verse

Watch and pray so that you will not fall into temptation (Matthew 26:41).

Calvary

Jesus was led away to be crucified at Calvary, outside the city of Jerusalem. He was whipped, beaten, made fun of and jeered at by the Roman soldiers. They forced him to wear a crown of thorns on his head so that he was already bleeding and tired before he reached the crucifixion site. Jesus was then nailed to the cross by his hands and feet and left to hang there in terrible pain until he died.

Salvation

Next Column

His suffering and death fulfilled a wonderful plan of salvation for his people. All sin must be punished by a holy God. The perfect Lord Jesus took the punishment for the sin of his people who trust in him. Even when he was being nailed to the cross, Jesus prayed to God, "Father forgive them for they do not know what they are doing." What love he showed.

P

Fulfilled from pages 85 & 88

Next Column

Gordon's Calvary: *A possible site of the crucifixion.*

Matthew 27:33 says that they took Jesus to be crucified at a place "called Golgotha (which means The Place of the Skull)."

Some people think that the rock in this photograph resembles a skull and could be the Golgotha referred to by Matthew.

The soldiers took Jesus' garment and cut it into four parts. Each of them took a piece. His coat was one complete piece of material. "Don't tear it," a soldier suggested. "Let's cast lots and let the winner take it all." That small detail had been foretold many years before in the book of Psalms. (Psalm 22.)

Jesus' mother Mary and some other women stood near the cross, watching what was happening. Jesus noticed his mother and his disciple John. "Look on John as your son now," he said to Mary. To John he said, "Treat Mary like your mother." John took Mary to live in his home from that day on.

Two other men, both criminals, were crucified with Jesus, one on either side of him. One complained to Jesus, "If you are really Christ, why can't you save yourself and us?" The other man was indignant. "How can you speak like that? We deserve this punishment but he has done nothing wrong."

He turned to Jesus and said "Remember me when you come to your kingdom."

Page 144

Jesus said, "Today you will be with me in heaven." This man believed in Jesus at the end of his life and received God's salvation.

Salvation

Page 141

From 12 noon until 3 o'clock darkness was over the whole land. Jesus was bearing the full punishment for the sin of all his people. In agony he called out, "My God, my God, why have you forsaken me?" When he called out, "I am thirsty," he was given a sponge soaked in vinegar. After Jesus had drunk the vinegar he cried, "It is finished."

Page 85

Just before he died he shouted with a loud voice,

"Father into your hands I commit my spirit."

Then the big curtain of the temple was torn in two from top to bottom.

There was an earthquake and the rocks were split in two.

These miracles amazed the soldiers. "Certainly, this man was the Son of God," they declared.

Fulfilled from Page 85

When they took Jesus' body down from the cross they did not break his legs because he was dead already. A soldier took a spear and thrust it into Jesus' side. Out poured blood and water.

That evening a rich man called Joseph went to Pilate and asked if he might bury Jesus' body in his own tomb. His request was granted, so with the help of Nicodemus, Joseph took Jesus body from the cross and wrapped it in a linen cloth. They carried the body through a garden and laid it carefully in the tomb, a cave cut out of the rock. A big stone was placed at the mouth of the cave, it was sealed and a guard was set to keep watch.

Fact File

Forgiveness: This means pardon for sin. We are forgiven by God only because of what Jesus did.

Memory Verse

Jesus said, 'But I, when I am lifted up from the earth, will draw all men to myself.' (John 12:32).

 Think Spot Wicked men were responsible for Jesus' death, but it was all in God's plan that he should die to save his people from their sins.

Resurrection

Very early in the morning on the first day of the week (Sunday or The Lord's day), Mary Magdalene and two other women came to the tomb where Jesus had been buried.

They wanted to anoint Jesus' body with spices. Their big concern was the heavy stone at the door of the tomb. Who would move it for them?

The Garden Tomb: Jerusalem

What a surprise they got when they reached the tomb. The stone was already rolled away. Mary Magdalene rushed off to tell the news to Peter and John. "Someone has taken away the Lord's body and I do not know where they have put him," she said.

The other two women crept into the tomb and saw two angels in dazzling white clothes. "Don't be afraid," one said. "I know you look for Jesus who was crucified. He is not here. He has risen. Go tell his disciples, especially Peter, that he has risen from the dead."

Peter and John ran to the tomb when they heard the news to see for themselves the linen clothes lying where Jesus had been.

Mary Magdalene came back to the garden weeping. She thought Jesus' body had been stolen. A man came to

☹ Page 146

speak to her. "Why are you crying?" he asked. "Who are you looking for?"

She thought the man was a gardener. "Sir," she said to him, "if you have taken him away, please tell me where you have laid his body."

"Mary," the man said to her. Mary, overjoyed, realised that the man was the risen Lord Jesus. "Master," she cried. ☺ Page 142

Mary ran with the good news to the disciples.

Jesus then appeared to all the disciples and to many others – at least 500.

Cleopas and his friend were walking from Jerusalem to Emmaus, talking about what had happened in Jerusalem.

Jesus himself came alongside them and walked with them. They didn't recognise him and thought he was a stranger. They were upset by Jesus' death but he explained to them from the Old Testament that Jesus had to suffer these things before he entered glory. 👁 Page 88

When they reached Emmaus they persuaded the man to stay for some food for it was late. When they sat down, Jesus took bread, blessed it and broke off a piece for each of them. Only then did they recognise the risen Lord Jesus. Immediately he vanished from their sight.

"That explains how we felt so excited when he spoke to us on the road, explaining the Scriptures to us," they said. They rushed back to Jerusalem to tell the disciples. "The Lord is risen indeed."

Some time later seven of the disciples went fishing on the Sea of Galilee. They fished all night but caught nothing.

The resurrection is a well attested fact. There is no doubt about it. He appeared bodily to:

Mary Magdalene

Other women

Peter

Ten disciples

Eleven disciples including Thomas

Two on the Emmaus Road

500 people

James and the apostles

As they came back to the beach, they noticed a man standing there.

"Have you anything to eat?" the man asked.

"No," they replied.

"Put your net down again," he said. When they did that, they caught a huge number of fish. John then recognised Jesus. "It is the Lord," he gasped. Peter jumped into the sea and rushed to the shore ahead of the boat.

On the shore Jesus had a fire lit with fish already cooking and some bread.

"Come and have something to eat," he said.

They all knew that this was Jesus.

 Memory Verse These are written that you may believe that Jesus is the Christ, the Son of God, and that by believing you may have life in his name (John 20:31). **Salvation** ☒ Page 143

Think Spot — Jesus conquered death by being raised from the dead. Those who trust in him need not be afraid of death. They too will rise again at the last day.

Ascension

The risen Lord Jesus was seen and recognised by many people during the forty days that he was in the world after his resurrection from the dead. During this time he taught his followers.

"Go into all the world," he told them, "and preach the gospel to everyone."

They went out of the city to the Mount of Olives. Jesus told his disciples that they would be his witnesses at home and in many far-off places, telling others the good news of the gospel.

He lifted up his hands to bless them, and he was lifted up into heaven, right through the clouds.

The disciples stood gazing up to heaven in astonishment. Two angels in white stood beside them and asked, "Why are you standing here looking up to heaven? Just as you have seen Jesus being taken up to heaven, he will return to earth one day."

The disciples worshipped God and went joyfully back to Jerusalem to start the work of preaching the gospel with new energy.

Page 31

Pentecost

On the feast day called the day of Pentecost the disciples were sitting together in a house. Suddenly there was a loud noise like a very strong wind. They all saw tongues of fire settling over each man's head.

Then they were all able to speak in many foreign languages. God, the Holy Spirit had come and given his power to each man to help him to preach the gospel to people of many nations. They were given the special title "apostle".

Many foreign visitors were in Jerusalem and when they heard Peter and the other Galilean men speaking in their own languages they were amazed. Many were astonished by God's power but others accused them of being drunk.

Peter stood up to explain. "These men are not drunk. The Holy Spirit has come to them. Let me tell you about Jesus. He did many wonderful miracles, but you took him and cruelly killed him. But he rose from the dead."

The people listening to Peter's sermon were very affected. "What must we do?" they asked.

Peter's Response:

Peter replied, "Repent and be baptised every one of you, in the name of Jesus Christ for the forgiveness of your sins. And you will receive the gift of the Holy Spirit. The promise is for you and your children and for all who are far off - for all whom the Lord our God will call" (Acts 2: 38-39).

Fact File

Acts: History book written by Luke, telling the story of Peter and Paul and other apostles.

Day of Pentecost: Fifty days after the Passover Feast (Leviticus 23:16), beginning of harvest thanksgiving.

Salvation

Page
145

Page
138

On that day about 3,000 people believed in the Lord Jesus Christ. Remember how Jesus had prayed on the cross that those crucifying him would be forgiven.

Lame Man Healed

One afternoon Peter and John went to the temple to pray. At the Beautiful Gate a lame man sat begging. He asked Peter and John for money. "I have no silver or gold," Peter replied, "but I will give you something else. In the name of Jesus Christ rise up and walk." He took him by the right hand and pulled him to his feet. Immediately he felt strength surging into his feet and ankles. He was able to walk for the first time ever. He went into the temple with Peter and John, jumping for joy and praising God. The people recognised him and could hardly believe that he was the same man who used to sit begging at the gate.

 Jesus told his followers to go into all the world and preach the Gospel to everyone. If we know the Good News of the Gospel we should pass it on to someone else.

 Memory Verse

The Lord added to their number daily those who were being saved (Acts 2:47).

Stephen

Stephen was a devout follower of Jesus. He looked after the daily distribution of food to the poor. He did many miracles through God's power, and spoke wisely. But one day he was falsely accused of blaspheming against God. He was seized and brought before the high court of the Jews. Several people told lies about him. When Stephen stood up to reply his face was shining like an angel. The Lord helped him to find the right words. Stephen reminded them of God's goodness to the Jewish nation in the past, and their rebellion against him. He boldly accused them of murdering the Lord Jesus. The priests were furious.

Stephen, full of the Holy Spirit, looked up to heaven and saw the Lord Jesus. "Look!" he said. "I see heaven open and Jesus standing at the right hand of God."

The Jewish priests were furious. Yelling at the tops of their voices, they dragged Stephen out of the city and killed him by hurling stones at him. "Lord Jesus, receive my spirit," Stephen prayed. "Do not hold this sin against them." How like Jesus' prayer on the cross.

Page 145

A man named **Saul** watched Stephen's stoning. He was guarding the coats the men had taken off. Saul had been born to Jewish parents in Tarsus in a country we now call Turkey. Saul was brought up to learn the law of God in great detail. He studied under a famous teacher called Gamaliel. When he grew up he also taught Jewish law and learned the trade of tent-making.

Conversion of Saul

Saul was violently opposed to Jesus and his followers. He did all he could to hurt the Christian people. He set off, with official letters of permission, to Damascus in the north. He planned to arrest followers of Jesus and take them back to Jerusalem to be punished or even killed. Near Damascus, around midday, a bright light shone from heaven. Saul threw himself to the ground, terrified. He heard a voice saying, "Saul, Saul, why are you persecuting me?" "Who are you Lord," Saul replied. "I am Jesus whom you are persecuting," came the reply. "It is dangerous for you to fight against

Fact File

Stoning: Hebrew method of capital punishment.

Fact File Page 54

Think Spot

Paul's conversion was dramatic. At first he hated Jesus and his followers. After he met Jesus on the road he loved and served him. What do you think about Jesus?

my power." The people with Saul saw the light and were afraid. Saul trembled with fear. "What do you want me to do?" "Go to Damascus and you will be told what to do."

Saul got up but when he opened his eyes he could see nothing. He had to be led by the hand into Damascus. For three days he was blind. He did not eat or drink. He stayed in a house in Straight Street, praying to God. God heard his prayers and sent Ananias to help him. Ananias had heard of Saul's bad reputation and was nervous. But he obeyed God and went to help Saul. "Brother Saul," he said, "the Lord Jesus, who spoke to you on the road, has sent me to you so that you may see again. You will be filled with the Holy Spirit too." Immediately he could see. He got up and was baptised to show that he believed in the Lord Jesus Christ. He then ate some food – the first for three days – and soon felt strong.

Saul preached powerfully in Damascus that Jesus is the Son of God. This upset the Jewish people so much that some were plotting to kill Saul. Word of this plot reached Saul and one dark night he was helped to escape by being lowered in a basket over the city wall. This was the start of Saul's new life as a follower of Jesus. His name was changed to **Paul**.

Page 146

Salvation

Page 146

Page 30

Memory Verse

Lord Jesus, receive my spiri (Acts 7:59).

Straight Street: Damascus

This is a photograph of Straight Street in Damascus which is still in existence today. Saul stayed there when he was blind and being looked after by a man named Judas. When God told Ananias to visit Saul he gave exact instructions about how to find him. 'Go to the house of Judas on Straight Street...' There is no detail, however small, that escapes the attention of the Lord God.

Peter's Adventures

Peter and the apostles did many wonderful miracles. He travelled round the country telling people the good news of the gospel. In Lydda he met a man who had been in bed for eight years, unable to walk. "Aeneas," he said to him, "Jesus Christ makes you whole. Get up and make your bed." He immediately was healed and many people believed in Jesus.

Dorcas

A lovely lady called Dorcas lived in the next town, Joppa. She loved Jesus and served him by making clothes for poor families.

Next Column

Next Column

Salvation

Next Column

Sadly Dorcas became ill and died. Her friends were so upset. They heard that Peter had healed a man in Lydda so they sent for him. When he arrived, the friends showed him the clothes that Dorcas had made for them. Then Peter asked them all to leave the room. He kneeled down and prayed. He then turned to Dorcas and said, "Get up." She opened her eyes and when she saw Peter she sat up. Peter took her hand and helped her out of bed. He called all her friends back. They were delighted to see her well again. News of this miracle spread through Joppa and many believed in Jesus.

Cornelius

North of Joppa in the town of Caesarea lived a Roman soldier called Cornelius. He was religious and prayed to God and gave to the poor. One day he had a vision. An angel came and said, "Send to Joppa for Peter to come to your house."

Cornelius sent two servants and a soldier to find Peter. They found him on the roof top of a house thinking about a vision he had received from the Lord. God, the Holy Spirit instructed Peter to go with these men. When Peter arrived he preached to Cornelius and his friends telling them that Jesus has followers from every nation. He told them about Jesus' miracles, his death and resurrection. "Everyone who believes in him receives forgiveness of sin," declared Peter. Cornelius and his friends believed and were filled with the Holy Spirit.

Salvation

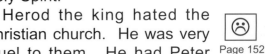

Page 148

Herod the king hated the Christian church. He was very cruel to them. He had Peter thrown into prison. The Christian friends were very concerned and prayed to God continually for him. Peter was fast asleep chained between two soldiers. The prison was locked and guarded. An angel came to the prison and woke Peter. "Get up quickly," he said. The chains fell from his hands. "Get dressed then follow me."

Page 152

Page 147

Joppa

Peter obeyed. They went past one guard and then another, right out into the street, God had delivered him from the prison.

Page 149

Some Christians had met at Mary's house to pray for Peter. Rhoda heard a knock on the door and ran to answer it. She heard Peter's voice but was so surprised that she did not open the door. Instead she ran back to tell the others. "Don't talk nonsense," they said. "It is Peter," she insisted. "I know his voice."

Peter kept knocking and eventually the door was opened and they all saw Peter. Their prayers had been wonderfully answered.

 Think Spot

Dorcas didn't just talk about doing good things she actually did them. It can be easy to be kind and helpful if you think you will get something in return. Ask God to give you a kind and gentle heart and to help you to be good and caring like Dorcas.

Memory Verse

Be kind and compassionate to one another, forgiving each other, just as in Christ God forgave you (Ephesians 4:32).

Fact File

Joppa: A seaside town known today as Jaffa.

Centurion: Cornelius was a centurion - in charge of 100 men.

Paul's First Missionary Journey

God sent Paul to many interesting places to preach the good news about Jesus Christ. On the first trip he went with Barnabas who had been his first friend in Jerusalem after his conversion, and a young man John Mark.

They travelled through the island of Cyprus preaching the gospel in the synagogues. They faced stiff opposition but God the Holy Spirit helped them to resist that and the governor of the island was so impressed by the teaching about the Lord that he believed in Jesus for himself.

Salvation

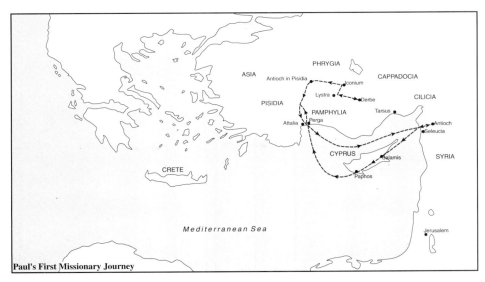

Page 150

John Mark left them at this point to go home. Paul and Barnabas travelled on to the area we now call Turkey. There they had many adventures. Some received them kindly but others chased them away.

At Lystra they met a crippled man, who had never been able to walk. He listened carefully to Paul's preaching. Paul looked at him and knew he had faith to be healed so he called out, "Stand up on your feet."

Immediately the man jumped up and started to walk.

The crowds of people watching were amazed but they foolishly thought that Paul and Barnabas were gods and wanted to worship them. This is against the first commandment God gave to his people.

Page 42 and Page 149 Memory Verse

This upset Paul and Barnabas very much. "We are just men like you," they protested. "Do not worship us. Worship the living God who made the heavens and earth and everything in it. God is the one who gives you all you need and will fill your heart with joy." Even with these words they had difficulty in stopping the crowd from sacrificing to them.

Before long the mood of the crowd had completely changed when some Jews started to speak against Paul and Barnabas. The crowd who had been worshipping Paul now began to hurl stones at him.

He was dragged out of the city and left for dead.

Some believers came to his aid and helped him back to town. The next day he and Barnabas left.

On their return journey they stopped off at various towns encouraging the people to remain true to the faith. "We must go through many hardships to enter the kingdom of God," explained Paul.

Paul's First Missionary Journey

Page 150
They appointed elders to look after each church and with prayer and fasting, committed them to the Lord before going on to the next place. Eventually they sailed back to Antioch and told the Christians there all that God had done through them. After some time they both wanted to make a return visit to the various church groups they had set up.

Barnabas wanted to take young John Mark with them but Paul objected as he had let them down before. So they decided to go separate ways. Barnabas accompanied by John Mark went back to Cyprus. Paul joined forces with Silas.

Antioch today

 Think Spot

Paul faced many dangers and difficulties when he was doing God's work. He did not give up. He persevered and asked God to help him.

 Memory Verse Page 42 You shall have no other gods except me (Exodus 20:3).

Fact File

Antioch: The followers of Jesus were called Christians first at Antioch.

Paul's Second Missionary Journey

Page 158

Paul, Silas and young Timothy went on a missionary trip to encourage the Christians and teach the people. The Holy Spirit guided them and prevented them from travelling to Bithynia so instead they went to the sea port of Troas. That night Paul had a vision. A man from Macedonia (Greece) pleaded, "Come over to Macedonia and help us." Immediately they sailed to Macedonia in Europe. God wanted them to preach the gospel there. When they reached Philippi they stopped for several days.

See below

On the Sabbath they went to the riverside where many women had gathered to pray. Paul preached to the group. One of the group, a woman called Lydia, was a business woman who sold beautiful purple cloth. She knew about God's word but on that day her heart was opened to respond quietly to Jesus Christ. She and her family were baptised and Paul and his friends, came to stay at her home.

Salvation

Page 151

One day on the way to the prayer meeting Paul met a slave girl who made money for her owners by telling fortunes. God used Paul to deliver her from the evil spirit, so that she no longer told fortunes. Her masters were angry. They dragged Paul and Silas to the market place and accused them of causing a disturbance in the town.

They were stripped and beaten and thrown in jail. The jailer put them in a cell and fastened their feet in stocks. But Paul and Silas were not sad. They prayed and sang praises to God. Everyone in the prison could hear them.

Page 154

Fact File

Roman Citizens: These people had special privileges. It was a crime to beat them.

Stocks: A painful clamp that kept the feet of the prisoner firmly fixed.

Suddenly an earthquake shook the prison. Doors flew open and all the chains came loose. The jailer grabbed a sword to kill himself. He thought his life would not be worth living if his prisoners escaped. Just in time Paul shouted, "Don't harm yourself. We're all here." The jailer called for lights and brought Paul and Silas out of the cell and asked, "Sirs, what must I do to be saved?"

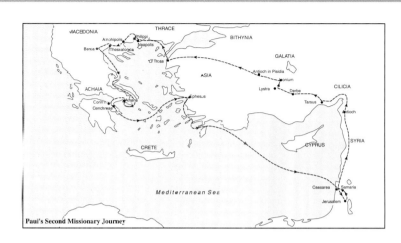

Paul's Second Missionary Journey

Corinth: Ruins of ancient temple

Think Spot

Conversion is when someone begins to believe in Jesus. This experience can happen in many ways. Lydia's conversion was quiet and gentle but the jailer's conversion was sudden and dramatic. God uses the best way for each person.

Memory Verse

Believe on the Lord Jesus Christ and you will be saved (Acts 16:31, KJV).

"Believe in the Lord Jesus Christ and you will be saved," Paul replied. Then they preached the good news of the gospel to the jailer and his family. They all believed and were baptised. The jailer washed their wounds and fed them well. The next day the judges ordered the release of Paul and Silas. But Paul said, "We are Roman citizens beaten and thrown in jail without trial. Let the judges escort us out of prison."

Salvation
X
Page 152

The judges, embarrassed to hear that Paul and Silas were Roman citizens, set them free and politely asked them to leave the city. Paul and Silas then went to meet with the Christians gathered in Lydia's house before continuing their travels.

On the journey they spoke God's word to many people – Jews in Thessalonica and Berea, philosophers in Athens. In Corinth Paul stayed with Priscilla and Aquila and worked at his tent making trade as well as preaching the gospel.

God also encouraged Paul by speaking to him in a dream. "Keep on speaking my message, I am with you. I have many people in this city." Paul stayed there teaching for a year and a half.

Bible Explorer

New Testament/History — Acts 19 – 21

Paul's Third Missionary Journey

Paul's preaching had great effect on those who heard him. In the Ephesus synagogue some objected strongly to what he said so he went to another hall. There he had daily discussions for two years. Many heard the word of God there and followed Jesus. Some who had formerly practiced evil sorcery gathered together all their evil scrolls and publicly burned them. God's word grew and spread in the town.

Salvation

X

Page 155

A silversmith called Demetrius stirred up trouble, however. He was annoyed that Paul's preaching had turned people away from worshipping idols. They no longer bought the silver shrines that he made. So with other silversmiths he caused a riot. They shouted abuse about Paul and his friends and would not listen to anyone.

☹

Page 153

Eventually the city clerk made them see sense. "They have done nothing to harm you. If you have any grievance, take it to the law courts in a civil manner. Don't start a riot." The crowd dispersed, but Paul decided to leave the town, and set off for Greece and Macedonia - preaching and encouraging along the way.

Troas

Paul and his companions stayed in Troas for a week. The evening before they were due to leave, Paul preached in an upstairs room. A boy called Eutychus sat on a window ledge listening. Paul had so much to say to the people before he would leave them that he talked until midnight. Eutychus was so sleepy, he drifted off into a deep sleep and fell right down to the ground from the upstairs window. He was picked up dead, but Paul came down and threw himself on the young man, putting his arms around him. "Don't be alarmed," he said. "He's alive!" Eutychus was brought back to life by the power of God! Everyone went back upstairs again, shared bread together and carried on speaking until dawn. Paul then had to leave and Eutychus went home safe and well.

Ephesus: Ruins of the Harbour Road

@ Page 152

Back to Jerusalem

Paul returned to Jerusalem and a warm welcome from the church, but

Page 21

evil men stirred up trouble and had Paul arrested. He was rescued from an angry mob by Roman soldiers who took him to the barracks.

"May I speak?" asked Paul. With the commander's permission he spoke to the crowd telling them his life story and how he was converted. The crowd listened quietly until he said, "The Lord told me to go far away to reach the Gentiles." This angered them and they shouted insults again. "Take him away," ordered the commander, "and flog him."

As they were about to beat Paul, he asked a soldier, "Is it legal for you to flog a Roman citizen who has not been found guilty?"

The soldier reported this to his commander who investigated. "I had to buy my citizenship," he told Paul. "But I was born a citizen," Paul replied. The commander was alarmed when he realised how badly he had treated Paul, a Roman citizen.

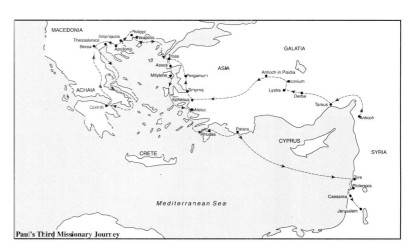

Paul's Third Missionary Journey

Evil men plotted to kill Paul but their plans were thwarted by Paul's nephew who heard about the scheme and warned Paul. The commander ushered Paul out of the city during the night to Caeserea to keep him safe. Paul ended up telling his story to one offical after another. Felix the governor listened for a bit but was afraid to deal with the matter. "I'll send for you again when it suits me," he said. Festus his successor discussed the matter with King Agrippa. Paul reasoned with them too but eventually the decision was taken. Paul must go to Rome. Caesar would deal with the matter.

Think Spot

Paul was not afraid of the important men he met like Felix, Festus and Agrippa. He preached the good news about Jesus Christ to them too.

Fact File

Caesar: The Roman ruler who had control over the land of Judea where Felix and then Festus was his governor.

Memory Verse

For it is by grace you have been saved, through faith, and this not from yourselves; it is the gift of God (Ephesians 2:8).

Paul Sails to Rome

Paul sailed for Rome in the charge of Julius, a Roman centurion. The ship landed at Sidon and Julius allowed Paul to visit some friends there. Their route then took them north of Cyprus. At Myra in Asia they changed ships. Progress was slow and difficult as the wind blew them off course. The journey became very dangerous.

Page 159 At Fair Havens harbour on the island of Crete, Paul warned Julius, "This voyage will end in disaster. We should stay here."

But Julius did not listen to Paul. He followed the wishes of the pilot and the ship owner and sailed on. In the middle of the Adriatic Sea they hit a big storm with hurricane force winds. The life boat was hoisted from the water to stop it being shattered. Cargo was thrown overboard to lighten the load. On day three they even threw over some of the ship's equipment. The storm was so fierce that they all gave up hope of being saved. Paul reminded them of his advice. "But don't despair," he urged. "No one will be lost. Only the ship will be destroyed. An angel told me that we will all live. I have faith in God that it will happen as he told me."

After fourteen nights at sea the sailors sensed that they were near land. They took soundings and discovered that the sea was shallower. They were in real danger of being wrecked on the rocks.

The sailors dropped four anchors from the stern of the boat and prayed for daylight. Some tried to escape on the lifeboat while pretending to work at the anchors. Page 155

Paul confronted Julius. "Unless these men stay with the ship, we will not be saved." So the lifeboat was tossed into the sea. Before dawn Paul urged everyone to eat something.

He took some bread, thanked God for it and the others took courage from him and did the same. Next Column When daylight came they saw a bay with a sandy beach. Before the ship reached the shore it stuck fast in a sand-bar. The ship was broken in pieces by the pounding waves.

Those who could swim jumped overboard and made for land. Others kept afloat on broken pieces of the ship. All reached land safely.

When they came ashore they discovered that the island was Malta. The people treated them kindly, building a big fire on the shore to warm them. Paul gathered up a pile of brushwood and as he put it on the fire a snake bit his hand. The Page 162 islanders thought this was a sign that he was an evil man. When Paul shook the snake off into the fire and suffered no harm, they changed their minds and thought he was a god! Paul and his party were well looked after by the chief official of Malta.

Many sick people including the official's father were healed of various diseases after Paul had prayed to God for them. Then after three months another ship was ready to set sail to Italy. At last Paul reached the city of Rome, where he was allowed to live by himself with soldiers to guard him.

 Page 156

He preached boldly in Rome and some who heard the gospel believed on the Lord Jesus Christ. For two years Paul was able to preach and teach about Jesus in his prison house.

Salvation Page 156

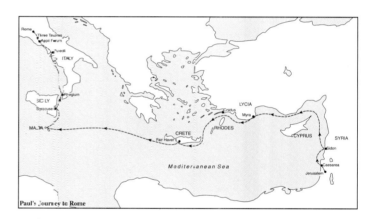

Paul's Journey to Rome

Fact File

When Paul was in Rome under house arrest he not only preached to those who visited him but he wrote letters to some churches and people. These letters are part of the Bible – Galatians, Ephesians, Philippians, Colossians, II Timothy, Philemon.

 Think Spot

When Paul was in danger he showed great courage and care for his fellow travellers. He trusted fully in God. When we are in difficult situations we should ask God to give us courage and faith in him.

Memory Verse

The Lord will keep you from all harm - he will watch over your life (Psalm 121:7).

Letters to the Churches from Paul

Paul wrote letters to different churches that he knew. They would have been read out to the congregations when they met together. The letters have important lessons for us today. Just one part of each letter is written here.

Salvation ☒ Page 158

Romans: Written to the Roman church this letter explains the Christian faith and points to Christ as the way of salvation. "The wages of sin is death, but the gift of God is eternal life in Christ Jesus our Lord," (Romans 6:23).

1 & 2 Corinthians: Paul wrote two letters to the Corinthian church. He lovingly tried to help them with their problems. "Love is patient, love is kind. It does not envy, it does not boast, it is not proud. It is not rude, it is not self-seeking, it is not easily angered, it keeps no record of wrongs. Love does not delight in evil but rejoices with the truth. It always protects, always trusts, always hopes, always perseveres," (1 Corinthians 13:4-7).

Galatians: The churches in Galatia which Paul had set up during his first missionary journey needed encouragement to follow Christ and not look back to old Jewish rituals. "The fruit of the Spirit is love, joy, peace, patience, kindness, goodness, faithfulness, gentleness and self-control. Against such things there is no law," (Galatians 5:22-23).

Ephesians: This letter to the Ephesian church tells of the oneness of God's people - united to Christ who gives each believer new life. "Be strong in the Lord and in his mighty power. Put on the full armour of God so that you can take your stand against the devil's schemes ... Take up the shield of faith with which you can extinguish all the flaming arrows of the evil one. Take the helmet of salvation and the sword of the Spirit which is the word of God. And pray in the Spirit on all occasions with all kinds of prayers and requests," (Ephesians 6:10-18).

Paragraph below

Philippians: Paul wrote this letter from prison but it is full of joy. "Rejoice in the Lord always. I will say it again: Rejoice," (Philippians 4:4); "Do not be anxious about anything, but in everything, by prayer and petition with thanksgiving, present your requests to God," (Philippians 4:6).

Page 157

"Whatever is true, whatever is noble, whatever is right, whatever is pure, whatever is lovely, whatever is admirable, if anything is excellent or praiseworthy, think about such things," (Philippians 4:8).

Colossians: Paul wrote the church in Colosse to warn them of false teaching. He

Page 160

emphasised the true Christian message. "So then, just as you received Christ Jesus as Lord, continue to live in him, rooted and built up in him, strengthened in the faith as you were taught, and overflowing with thankfulness," (Colossians 2:6-7).

1 & 2 Thessalonians: Paul wrote twice to the church at Thessalonica which he founded during his second missionary journey. He tells them how thankful he is to hear of their faith and love. He also answered questions about the return of Jesus Christ to the world. "Be joyful always; pray continually; give thanks in all circumstances, for this is God's will for you in Christ Jesus," (1 Thessalonians 5:16-18).

Thessalonica: A view from the walls

 Think Spot

Paul prayed that each of these churches would be given grace and Memory Verse peace from God. Grace is God's gift of mercy which is undeserved by every sinner but which God loves to give.

 Memory Verse

Grace and peace to you from God our Father and the Lord Jesus Christ (Philippians 1:2). Think Spot

Fact File

Epistles: This is another name for the letters of the New Testament. There are twenty-one letters in the New Testament. Thirteen were written by Paul, some to church groups and some to individuals.

Church: The word used here does not mean a building but the group of believers in Christ who met together to worship him.

Letters to the Churches: Romans; 1 & 2 Corinthians; Galatians; Ephesians; Philippians; Colossians; 1 & 2 Thessalonians.

Letters to Other People

1 & 2 Timothy

Paul wrote two letters to a young believer, Timothy, who had helped him spread the gospel. Paul gives Timothy good advice for a Christian and a church leader.

👁 Page 150

"Continue in what you have learned and have become convinced of, because you know those from whom you learned it, and how from infancy you have known the holy Scriptures which are able to make you wise for salvation through faith in Jesus Christ," 2 Timothy 3:14–15.

Salvation ☒
Page 159

Paul chose Timothy to be one of his assistants and to travel on a missionary journey with him. Timothy was brought up in Lystra. His mother was Jewish and his father was from Greece. Timothy's mother Eunice and his grandmother Lois loved and trusted God and taught Timothy the ways of God in the Scripture from his earliest years. However,

Timothy was not a very strong person and Paul advised him to take a little wine now and again as medicine to help his digestion.

Timothy was also timid by nature but Paul encouraged him in his work of spreading the Gospel. He told him that training to be godly was far more important than physical training.

Even though he was young Timothy had to set an example for the church. In the way he spoke and lived, he showed them love and his faith in God and his desire to be pure and holy.

Fact File

Letters to Individuals: Paul wrote some letters to individuals these are: Timothy; Titus and Philemon.

Philemon: The letter to Philemon was written personally by Paul – not dictated to a scribe or secretary. He was asking a special favour.

Titus: Paul writes to his friend Titus, a pastor on the island of Crete. He gives him good advice about godly behaviour and wise ruling in the church. "The grace of God that brings salvation has appeared to all men. It teaches us to say 'No' to ungodliness and worldly passions, and to live self-controlled, upright and godly lives in this present age," (Titus 2:11-12).

Crete - Fair Haven's Harbour: Paul wrote to Titus who lived on the island of Crete but if you look back to page 154 and Paul's journey to Rome you will see that Paul stopped off here before continuing the journey that resulted in the disastrous shipwreck on Malta.

Paul tells Titus that a good church leader should:

Be blameless
Be a husband of one wife 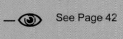 See Page 42
Control his children well
Not be quick tempered
Not be a drunkard
Not be violent ——— 👁 See Page 42
Not be dishonest ——— 👁 See Page 42
Be hospitable
Love what is good
Be self-controlled
Be upright
Be holy
Be disciplined
Be helpful to others
Be encouraging.

Philemon: Philemon was a wealthy Christian in Colosse. He had a large house with slaves. One slave, Onesimus, ran away after stealing from him. This was a serious offence worthy of severe punishment. Onesimus fled to Rome where he met Paul and heard God's way of salvation from him. He came to trust in the Lord Jesus too.

Salvation

☒

Page 160

Paul wrote to Philemon, asking him to forgive Onesimus and accept him as a Christian brother. Paul offered to pay anything that Onesimus owed. This letter shows how the gospel affects and changes people's lives.

Think Spot

Paul asked Philemon to forgive Onesimus who had wronged him. Is there someone you need to forgive? How can you show forgiveness?

Memory Verse

All Scripture is God-breathed and is useful for teaching, rebuking, correcting and training in righteousness (2 Timothy 3:16).

More Letters

Hebrews

We do not know who wrote this letter to the Hebrews or Jewish Christians, but he used the Old Testament Scriptures to point the readers to Jesus Christ. Chapter 11 shows how people from Israel's history did amazing things by faith, i.e. Abel, Enoch, Noah. We are urged to be faithful too.

> "Since we are surrounded by such a great cloud of witnesses, let us throw off everything that hinders and the sin that so easily entangles and let us run with perseverance the race marked out for us. Let us fix our eyes on Jesus, the author and perfecter of our faith, who for the joy set before him endured the cross, scorning its shame, and sat down at the right hand of the throne of God. Consider him who endured such opposition from sinful men, so that you will not grow weary and lose heart," (Hebrews 12:1–3).

James

James, a half-brother of Jesus, wrote to God's people all over the world with good advice about how a Christian should behave.

> "Be quick to listen, slow to speak and slow to become angry" (James 1:19–20).
> "The wisdom that comes from heaven is first of all pure; then peace-loving, considerate, submissive, full of mercy and good fruit, impartial and sincere," (James 3:17).

1 & 2 Peter

The disciple Peter wrote two letters to the Christians on Asia Minor (now Turkey). He wanted to encourage them because they were suffering persecution for their faith.

> "If you suffer for doing good and endure it this is commendable before God. To this you were called, because Christ suffered for you, leaving you an example that you should follow," (1 Peter 2:20–21).
>
> "He himself bore our sins in his body on the tree, so that we might die to sins and live for righteousness, by his wounds you have been healed," (1 Peter 2:24).

Salvation

Page 161

> "Cast all your anxiety on God because he cares for you," (1 Peter 5:7).

Page 161

> "Grow in the grace and knowledge of our Lord and Saviour Jesus Christ," (2 Peter 3:18).

1, 2 & 3 John

The apostle John wrote three letters One to a church, one to a Christian woman and her children and the third to Gaius. The first letter encourages the reader to live in fellowship with God, Jesus Christ, and with each other.

> **Salvation** ☒ Next Column
>
> "If we walk in the light, as he is in the light, we have fellowship with one another, and the blood of Jesus his Son purifies us from all sin," (1 John 1:7).
>
> "How great is the love the Father has lavished on us that we should be called children of God," (1 John 3:1).
>
> "Let us not love with words or tongue but with actions and in truth," (1 John 3:18).

The second letter is very short teaching the lady and her family about Christian hospitality.

> "And this is love; that we walk in obedience to his commands. As you have heard from the beginning, his command is that you walk in love," (2 John 6).

The third letter to Gaius is similar and is also very short. It is a friendly and encouraging letter.

> "I have no greater joy than to hear that my children are walking in the truth" (3 John 4).

Jude

Jude, one of the half-brothers of Jesus, wrote this letter to those who were loved by God the Father and kept by Jesus Christ. He warns against false teachers who might harm their Christian faith.

"But you, dear friends, build yourselves up in your most holy faith and pray in the Holy Spirit. Keep yourselves in God's love as you wait for the mercy of our Lord Jesus Christ to bring you to eternal life" (Jude 20–21).

Page 22

Salvation ☒

Page 162

Fact File

> **Faith:** This is a firm belief or trust in God.

> **More letters:** Hebrews, James, 1 & 2 Peter, 1, 2 & 3 John & Jude.

> **Written To:** The letters written by James, Peter, John, and Jude were to different Christians and groups of Christians.

 Memory Verse

God is love (1 John 4:16).

 Think Spot

We love God because God first loved us. How can you show love to others and in what ways do others show love to you? How has God shown you that he loves you?

Revelation

John wrote the book of Revelation while he was a prisoner for his faith on the island of Patmos in the Mediterranean Sea.

Pages 88-95

This is a prophetic book. Like the prophetic books in the Old Testament it tells what God has done in the past, what he is saying to his people at present and what he is going to do in the future. John explains how the Lord God spoke to him in a vision and told him to write it down. What he wrote is the book of Revelation.

God had special messages for each of the seven churches of Asia – Ephesus, Smyrna, Pergamum, Thyatira, Sardis, Philadelphia and Laodicea.

He commended the church at Ephesus for many good qualities but one thing was wrong - they did not love God as they had at first.

God accused the church at Laodicea of being lukewarm and apathetic not realising their miserable state. He appealed to them in a loving way.

Salvation
Page 12

"Behold I stand at the door and knock. If anyone hears my voice and opens the door, I will come in and dine with him and he with me," (Revelation 3:20, KJV).

Revelation is full of word pictures and symbols. The Lamb is the symbol used for the Lord Jesus Christ which reminds us of John the Baptist pointing to Jesus the Lamb of God who takes away the sin of the world.

Page 13

The Acropolis at Smyrna

Praise is given continually to Jesus in heaven by angels and all living creatures. "Worthy is the Lamb who was slain, to receive power and wealth and wisdom, and strength and honour and glory and praise," (Revelation 5:12).

God showed John how he would defeat evil and sin through Christ. Satan will be totally defeated. God's faithful people will be blessed with a new heaven and a new earth.

Seven Churches of Asia

John saw a vision of heaven and he described what he saw. In heaven there will be no tears, no death, no sorrow, no crying, no pain. (Revelation 21:4.) The city wall was of jasper, a precious stone: the city was made of gold. The foundations of the city adorned with all kinds of precious stones – jasper, sapphire, chalcedony, emerald, sardonyx, sardius, chrysolite, beryl, topaz, chrysoprase, jacinth and amethyst. The twelve gates were made of pearls. The street was of pure gold. (Revelation 21:18-21.) There was no temple in the city because the Lord Almighty and the Lamb (Jesus) are the temple. There was no need for sun or moon because the glory of God illuminated it. (Revelation 21:22-23.) Nothing wicked will enter heaven - only those whose names are written in the Lamb's Book of Life.

The island of Patmos

Memory Verse

Whoever is thirsty, let him come; and whoever wishes, let him take the free gift of the water of life (Revelation 22:17).

Think Spot

We are told in the book of Revelation that the Lord Jesus will return one day. He will judge the world and take his own people to be with himself. That gives the Christian hope for the future. We need to be faithfully waiting for him.

Fact File

Revelation: A Book of prophecy. It tells what God revealed to John in visions.

Holy City: Heaven is called the Holy City in Revelation.

F.A.Q.

(Frequently Asked Questions)

What is the Bible?

The Bible is God's Word. He has recorded it carefully for us and wants us to read and study it. We should pray that God would help you to understand what you read. It is divided into different sections.

Old Testament	**New Testament**
Law	Gospels
History	History
Poetry	Epistles
Prophecy	Prophecy

Why is there an Old Testament and a New Testament?

The Bible is divided into two sections called the Old Testament and the New Testament. The Old Testament has 39 books originally written in the Hebrew language. The New Testament has 27 books originally written in Greek. The Old Testament is a record of God's Word and promises to Abraham and the prophets. The New Testament shows us how these promises were fulfilled. The Old Testament records God's promise of a Messiah. The New Testament shows how Jesus Christ is the promised Messiah, God's Son, our hope of salvation.

How do you find your way around the Bible?

There are sixty-six books in total throughout the whole Bible. It can be a bit daunting when you first try to read the Bible for yourself. However, here are one or two points to remember:

Chapters and Verses: Each book of the Bible is divided into chapters and each chapter is divided into verses. This makes it easier for us to find a specific sentence in the book.

Regular study: The best way to understand the Bible is to study it regularly. The more you read the Bible, the more you will discover what God wants to say to you. It won't take long before you remember that in Romans 3:23 Paul warns about sin and that John 3:16 tells you about the love of God. It is important that we think about what we read and obey what God is telling us in the Bible. "Meditate on it day and night, so that you may be careful to do everything written in it," (Joshua 1:8).

Why should we read the Bible?

* The Bible gives us guidance about all the important issues of life.

* It is truth.

* It tells us the good news of salvation through Jesus Christ.

*It helps you to grow spiritually as a stronger Christian.

*God tells us to read the Bible. So it is our duty to do this.

*God has given us his word. It is a privilege to read it.

* Many Christians today do not have a copy of God's Word, the Bible, for themselves so we should read God's word and be thankful for it.

Do you always start to read the Bible at the beginning?

Genesis is a very interesting and exciting book. However a good way to read the Bible is to read a part of the New Testament and a part of the Old Testament as well as some verses from a Psalm. It is a good idea to take a notebook and keep track of what you have read. Always pray before you start. Ask God to help you understand and obey his word.

Is the Bible still relevant for today?

Of course it is! People haven't changed that much. We still have the same problems and make the same mistakes that Adam and Eve made in the Garden of Eden. We still need to obey God's commands. Just think about how much hurt, sadness and heartache would be avoided if we simply obeyed God's word.

The Bible is crucially relevant for today. It is relevant to every life. Each person is under God's command whether they believe in the Lord Jesus Christ or not. There is a day in every person's life when he or she will have to come face to face with God. The Bible tells us how to be ready for that day. The Bible tells us that if we believe in the Lord Jesus Christ we will be saved. The Bible is like a lamp that guides you through the darkness. The Bible guides you through life and shows you how to obey God.

Those who believe in the Lord Jesus Christ will spend eternity with him. Those who do not believe in the Lord Jesus Christ will be separated from him for ever in eternal punishment.

Character Index

Memory Verse Index

General Index